FISKE

250

words every
high school
graduate
needs to know

SECOND EDITION

D1059238

FISKE

250

words every
high school
graduate
needs to know

SECOND EDITION

EDWARD B. FISKE
JANE MALLISON AND DAVID HATCHER

 sourcebooks

YA
428
Fiske QB $9.00/8.00

Published by Sourcebooks, Inc.
P.O. Box 4410, Naperville, Illinois 60567-4410
(630) 961-3900
Fax: (630) 961-2168
www.sourcebooks.com

The Library of Congress has catalogued the first edition as follows:

Fiske, Edward B.
  Fiske 250 words every high school graduate needs to know / by Edward B. Fiske, Jane Mallison, and David Hatcher.
      p. cm.
  1. Vocabulary. 2. High school graduates—Language. I. Mallison, Jane. II. Hatcher, David. III. Title. IV. Title: Fiske two-hundred fifty words every high school graduate needs to know.
  PE1449.F5529 2009
  428.1—dc22
                                        2008048509

        Printed and bound in the United States of America.
                VP 10 9 8 7 6 5 4 3 2 1

contents

introduction

Chances are that you already know lots of words—probably tens of thousands. And now you are about to learn even more.

Not that we blame you—obviously, we're glad you're enlarging your hoard of words. You can probably already reel off some excellent reasons for learning more words: people with rich vocabularies make higher grades, score better on most standardized tests, and go on to be more successful in their chosen careers. They're also more interesting to talk to.

All these are valid reasons for expanding and refining your vocabulary. We'd like to add a couple more that we find equally valid.

One is that learning new words actually makes you smarter. You don't just *seem* smarter, you *are* smarter—you know more. Oliver Wendell Holmes, Jr., was right when he said a mind stretched by a new idea never goes back to its original dimensions. What's true for ideas is true for words. When you learn the word *symbiosis*, you become linked to the knowledge that plants and animals have worked out some fascinating and mutually beneficial ways to help each other—from the bird that cleans food fragments from the alligator's teeth to the tiny mite that clings to the bottom of an ant's foot (getting a bit of food from the ant's system, and perhaps serving as an athletic shoe to cushion the host's soles).

But getting smarter through learning words isn't limited to the acquisition of technical terms. As a friend once said, "If you know the names of the wildflowers, you're more likely to see them." That principle works for words as well. Once you learn the adjective *louche*, for example, you'll be able to recognize, to pinpoint, a variety of decadent slyness that you might earlier have tossed in the catchall basket labeled *weird*.

Here's one more reason, often overlooked but for us among the most important—you can learn words for the pure pleasure of it, for the joy of discovery, of finding out what the words mean, how they sound, maybe when they were born, where they come from, and how they've changed over the years. (Did you know a *bonfire* was once a *bone fire*?)

Isn't it a pleasure to know that there's a word for the pesky person who delights in catching others' errors—and triumphantly pointing them out? That person's a *doryphore* (DOR-a-fore). Or what about the fact that *crapulous* describes someone with a hangover?

And you doubtless know someone who talks too much—way too much. The person who goes on and on, sending out a seemingly unending flow of words, is suffering (or making us suffer) from *logorrhea* (LOG-uh-REE-uh).

So you have lots of reasons for expanding and deepening your vocabulary, and the words we've chosen for this book run the gamut. We think they'll help you satisfy all your reasons for learning new words, and that you'll find them interesting, useful, and fun.

Feel free to dive into this book anywhere you like, but

if you start at the beginning, you'll recognize a pattern of four chapters organized by themes, followed by a grab bag chapter, and a quiz over five chapters. If you complete the entire book (congratulations!), you'll have encountered two hundred words in the thematic chapters, learned fifty from the grab bag chapters, and taken five quizzes to reinforce your confidence that you've mastered them all.

This book follows the style and format of its parent book, *Fiske WordPower*, which contains one thousand words.* So when you're ready for lots more, move on to *Fiske WordPower*, by Edward B. Fiske, Jane Mallison, and Margery Mandell (Sourcebooks, 2006). You'll find hundreds of new words there—some practical, some intriguing, some both— and you'll recognize a few familiar friends you first met here.

---

* We've also written a sibling book with a completely different set of words, *Fiske 250 Words Every High School Freshman Needs to Know*. The words there are slightly easier than those in the book you're holding now—take a look.

1
aggressive words

"Comin'-at-ya!" That's, more or less, the literal meaning of "aggressive." Whether actual or just implied, the words below all concern some kind of attack, whether physical or verbal.

1. Scathe (rhymes with *bathe*)

This means "to harm or injure" and comes into English from Old Norse; those Vikings knew a thing or two about scathing. Today, you'll see it mostly in the two forms illustrated below.

- *While Henrik would never hit a member of his family, his **scathing** comments are brutal enough.*

- *The powerful force of Hurricane Katrina left no resident of New Orleans **unscathed**.*

2. Lacerate (LASS-er-ate)

This word refers to ripping or tearing, whether literal or figurative.

- *The pit-bull attack left Jeff with deep **lacerations** on his shin.*

- *The English translation of Jonathan Swift's self-written Latin epitaph refers to death as the only place* *where his heart would not be **lacerated** by a fierce indignation.*

3. Disparage (dis-PAIR-idge)

Though not as cruel as scathe or lacerate, this verb refers to a withering belittlement of someone or something. (The root word is related to the word *peer,* so if you're *dis-peered,* you're being made less of an equal than the speaker.)

- *Because Angela is insecure about her abilities, she finds it important to **disparage** the ideas of others, even before they've been given a hearing.*

- *Martin's **disparagement** of Bethany's attempts to make him happy gradually led to their break-up.*

4. Deride (de-RIDE)

Akin in meaning to *disparage,* this verb contains the additional tinge of meaning "scornful laughter."

- *In Shakespeare's comedy* A Midsummer Night's Dream, *Helena, ignorant of the magic potion put onto the eyes of Lysander and Demetrius, feels sure their declarations of love are attempts to **deride** her.*

- *"I'd rather have you make a straightforward attack on me than to treat my ideas with such **derision** in our staff meetings," asserted Randolph nervously to his supervisor.*

5. Temerity (tem-ER-it-ee)

From the Latin word meaning rash, this noun means "extreme boldness." Someone with temerity exhibits a foolish disregard for danger. There is actually an adjective form of the word, **temerarious**, but using this uncommon form would be a little bit audacious.

- *Oliver Twist had the **temerity** to ask for some more porridge when he knew the directors of the orphanage were determined to feed the boys as little as possible.*

- *It took a lot of **temerity** for the soldier to cross No Man's Land in the middle of a skirmish.*

In Shakespeare's comedy A Midsummer Night's Dream, *Helena, ignorant of the magic potion put onto the eyes of Lysander and Demetrius, feels sure their declarations of love are attempts to **deride** her.*

6. Diatribe (DYE-ah-tribe)

The root of the Greek word diatribe or "learned discourse" is *diatribein*, which means "to consume or wear away." In English, the noun means "a bitter, abusive lecture."

- *Stalin's speech was a furious **diatribe**, harshly critical of his political opponents.*

- *Xiao Xiao's cutting humor and brutal sarcasm made each of her movie reviews a hilarious **diatribe** against contemporary culture.*

7. Animus (AN-i-muss)

In its general meaning this noun expresses the idea of a hostile disposition, ill will toward someone. (In Jungian psychology the word describes masculine aspects of a female's unconscious.) The noun form is **animosity**.

- *"Why do all of your remarks to me have such an **animus**? I haven't done anything to deserve this jeering," said the fed-up Malcolm.*

- *The comic book character **Animus** deserves his name, for he is indeed a hatemonger and expresses **animosity** toward others.*

8. Excoriate (ex-CORE-ee-ate)

From the Latin word that means "to take off the skin," this verb means not only literally "to remove the skin" but "to censure strongly," as if flaying with words.

- *Simon's brutality as a talent show judge was so severe that contestants would often burst into tears as he **excoriated** them for the mistakes they had made during their performances.*

- *When Mara fell from her bike, her ankle was cut and her knee was **excoriated**.*

9. Emasculate (e-MASK-u-late)

In its literal sense it means "to castrate." Its more common figurative sense means "to weaken," "to deprive of strength," but you need to be sensitive to the original sense of the word. It would be laughable to refer to "emasculating the Miss America pageant by not televising it."

- *Jesse Jackson's crude remark about the then presidential candidate was reported by many newspapers as his wish to **emasculate** Barack Obama.*

- *Cutting the funds for the enforcement of the provisions of the bill completely **emasculated** its potential force.*

10. Flay (rhymes with *play*)

As with *emasculate*, *flay* has a particularly cruel literal meaning—here, the verb means "to strip the skin off someone." It's also more frequently used in the figurative sense of stinging with strong verbal criticism.

- *Apollo cruelly **flayed** Marsyas for daring to challenge him to a match of musical talent.*

- *"Was it not enough that he fired me?" asked David. "Did he really need to **flay** me with a recitation of all the flaws he perceived in my character?"*

2 fighting words

Maybe it doesn't speak well of human society, but the fact is that almost all languages have lots of words related to fighting. Here are some oft-used English ones.

1. Bellicose (BELL-ih-kose)

From the Latin root for "war," this adjective is about as hostile as you can get. Like *belligerent* (see # 7), it means "warlike."

- *The **bellicose** Mohawk Indians were quick to use their hatchets on the white settlers.*

- *Eager to fight, the **bellicose** reporter documented all of the instances of discrimination in the corporation's hiring policies.*

2. Agonistic (agg-un-ISS-tik)

This term doesn't carry the negative charge of *bellicose*. It comes from the Greek word for "struggle" (we get *agony* from it), and referred to participants in ancient Greek athletic contests. Although not common today, it's sometimes used as an adjective (following the noun) to refer to a person engaged in some kind of contest or struggle. And of course an **antagonist** is the person who's in opposition to a **protagonist**—terms we often use in literature.

- *John Milton's poem* Samson **Agonistes** *deals with the struggles of the Biblical hero Samson against his Philistine opponents.*

- *In the play* Oedipus Rex, *the title character is the* **protagonist** *and Creon, his brother-in-law, is the* **antagonist**.

3. Contentious (kon-TENCH-us)

To say some people are contentious doesn't mean they're likely to fight. It does mean that they're argumentative, not given to ready (or quiet) acceptance of views contrary to their own. In short, they like to **contend**.

- *A captain with a* **contentious** *crew has an ocean of misery.*

- *Don't be so* **contentious;** *why must you argue with everyone about everything?*

4. Pugnacious (pug-NAY-shus)

The pugnacious person blends some qualities of contention and bellicosity. Think of the street bully, ready to quarrel or fight, depending on the situation. The noun form is **pugnacity**.

- *That boy is really* **pugnacious,** *always getting into scraps and scuffles with his schoolmates.*

- *Given his* **pugnacity,** *we may expect him to grow up to be a* **pugilist** *(a boxer).*

5. Fractious (FRAK-shus)

Although someone who is fractious is considered unruly or a troublemaker, the adjective also means "peevish" or "cranky." It doesn't quite mean "stubborn," but the word does suggest an unwillingness to respect authority.

- The **fractious** child refused to finish her roast beef and spinach even though her father insisted.

- "Your **fractiousness** is another explanation of your lack of team spirit," said the coach, referring to Ian's refusal to sit on the bench for the ninth inning.

John Milton's poem Samson Agonistes *deals with the struggles of the Biblical hero Samson against his Philistine opponents.*

6. Truculent (TRUCK-you-lunt)

Think of a brooding, lowering person who seems to exude meanness and belligerence. Truculent can be used to describe speech and actions as well as people.

- Moose, the bouncer, appeared **truculent,** but his threatening manner was just an act.

- A fight erupted after the heat and heavy traffic brought out the worst in two **truculent** travelers.

7. Belligerent (beh-LIJ-er-ent)

Here's a strong adjective that means "aggressive" or "engaged in warfare." It comes from the Latin word that means "to wage war," the same root for *bellicose*. The noun form is **belligerence**.

- *By 1939, there could be no mistaking Germany's **belligerence** towards its neighbors.*

- *The boys in Mr. Sullivan's eighth-grade class were so **belligerent** that he had to separate their desks in the classroom.*

8. Obstreperous (ob-STREP-or-us)

From the Latin word that means "to make a noise against," this adjective means "aggressively and noisily defiant." People who are obstreperous make no bones about their obduracy. The noun form is **obstreperousness**.

- ***Obstreperous** by nature, Arthur threw a tantrum when his mother insisted that he put his pet ferret in the cage before joining the family for dinner.*

- *"I will not stand for your childish **obstreperousness**, Tom," Aunt Polly said firmly. "I asked you to help me paint the fence and if you continue to ignore me you'll have to paint the neighbor's fence too."*

9. Jingoist (JIN-go-ist)

This person may or may not be bellicose, truculent, or belligerent—not personally, anyway. The fighting he favors is to be done by his country's armed forces, not himself. The origin of the term is a bellicose music hall song that used "by jingo" as a frequent refrain; "jingo" was an obvious substitute for the taking in vain of the name of Jesus. The adjective form is **jingoistic**.

- *She worried constantly about all the **jingoistic** comments in regard to the Middle East.*

- *The ambassador tried to persuade the **jingoists** in the administration to give diplomacy a fair chance.*

10. Casus belli (KAY-sus BELL-eye)

Literally the Latin phrase for "the cause of war," a casus belli may be either an act or event that brings on a declaration of war, or—and this is important—something that is used as an excuse for military action.

- *The attack on Pearl Harbor was a clear **casus belli** for the U.S. entry into World War II.*

- *Many people believed that the talk of weapons of mass destruction was a fabricated **casus belli,** and not the real reason for action.*

3 flabby words

Tired, lazy, bored, or boring: this is a dull spectrum of feelings, but there's a fine array of words to express these sensations.

1. Ennui (ahn-WE)

This noun is a French import that refers to boredom or listlessness. If you're bored, you can at least give a Gallic shrug to express your state.

- *Jean Paul had planned to drop by Les Deux Magots in the afternoon for an aperitif, but once **ennui** set in, he merely sat quietly in his room listening to Edith Piaf songs.*

- *The gray sky and cold wind fed into Annette's sense of **ennui**, and the warm gloves and umbrella she had planned to purchase that afternoon remained on the shelves of the store.*

2. Inertia (in-ER-shuh)

This noun expresses a lack of motivation or an inability to change or to act. It can refer to a single individual or to a larger group such as a company or a country. The adjective form is **inert**.

- *After Willy lost his job, a profound sense of **inertia** overcame him and made it difficult to start looking for other work.*

- *The crowd watched in horror as the boxer lay **inert** in the center of the ring after the punch to the head.*

3. Phlegmatic (fleg-MAT-ik)

Here is an adjective describing a person who is slow to act, slow to get angry—more or less the far extreme from temperamental. While it can convey the positive sense of "calm," today it more often has a negative feel, possibly as suggested by the feel of a throat full of phlegm. (Word historians may enjoy knowing the long pedigree of this concept: as early as 400 BCE it was regarded as one of four basic "humors" or temperaments.)

- *Sarah likes to stir up an occasional feeling of jealousy in her boyfriends, but Ned's **phlegmatic** nature has conferred immunity on him thus far.*

- *The stereotype of a certified public accountant as somewhat **phlegmatic** certainly does not apply to Mel: he may crunch numbers all day, but on the weekend he skydives and bungee jumps.*

4. Feckless (FECK-less)

If you're feckless, you lack vitality and energy. Another possible shade of meaning describes someone who has energy but who fails to think about how his or her actions affect others. (The *feck* in feckless derives from the word *effect*.)

- *The new manager was hired because of impressive credentials, but his actual performance thus far has been rather **feckless**.*

- *Felicia was at first pleased to receive a call from her former boyfriend, but she truly had no interest in comforting him on the departure of a **feckless** new love interest.*

5. Torpid (TOR-pid)

If you're torpid, you have no energy. If you're a certain kind of animal, you might be hibernating, but if you're a plain old human being, you've let yourself get bored stiff. And that's what the Latin root means.

- *"So far as I know," said Jack, school expert on music of the last twenty-five years, "the only song with '**torpor**' in the lyrics is 'Like the Weather' by 10,000 Maniacs."*

- *Sean had promised his parents he'd clean out the garage on Saturday afternoon, but the sight of piled-up, rusting yard equipment and stacks of old copies of the Saturday Evening Post put him into a **torpid** frame of mind, and he took a nap instead.*

*"Your looks are okay," was Stanley Kowalski's rather **tepid** endorsement of Blanche Dubois's need for confirmation of her appeal.*

6. Lassitude (LASS-ih-tude)

Another noun for emotional fatigue or a dreamy, lazy mood, *lassitude* comes from the Latin word for "weary."

- *As the whispered phrase "Nichols is coming" went from cubicle to cubicle, workers interrupted their state of **lassitude** to assume the time-honored posture of looking busy when the boss approached.*

- *Jess had studied so hard for her exams that the end of exam week found her in a state of complete **lassitude**, barely able to do more than reach toward her bedside table for her mug of cocoa.*

7. Jaded (JAY-ded)

This condition of world-weariness may come from overfamiliarity or overindulgence in something originally pleasant. The word has nothing to do with the gemstone jade, but derives from an old word for a broken-down or useless horse.

- *Having a world-famous chef for a grandfather had given little Morgan a prematurely **jaded** attitude toward food. At ten he was heard to utter, "Fish quenelles? Again?"*

- *Those who are overly self-indulgent pay the price of becoming **jaded**, unable to enjoy exotic travel or fancy clothing that would delight most people.*

8. Doldrums (DOLE-drums)

If you're in the doldrums, you're feeling purposeless, without energy. In geographical terms, you're like the region of the ocean near the equator that is characterized by the absence of wind. (If you've read Samuel Taylor Coleridge's poem "The Rime of the Ancient Mariner," you've read about the nautical Doldrums.) The first syllable of the word comes from the adjective *dull*, and that's just how you feel.

- *Rosemary encouraged Julie to join in her economic venture, believing that a new partner could help shake the once-thriving business out of the **doldrums**.*

- *Some people are energized by complete freedom from supervision, but others get the **doldrums** when they have unstructured time on their hands.*

9. Stagnant (STAG-nunt)

It can happen to a pond, to a person, or to an abstraction such as the national economy. Wherever **stagnation** hits, there's an absence of vitality.

- *Toxic waste dumped into Hopewell Pond has transformed that sparkling body of water into a sadly **stagnant** pool.*

- *"Are you going to **stagnate** here at home all summer?" Mr. Crossman yelled at his teenaged son. "Get a job, take a class!"*

10. Tepid (TEP-id)

This adjective can literally describe a liquid that is "lukewarm, neither hot nor cold." It's also used figuratively, always negatively, to describe a "so-so" attitude.

- *The support offered to Mr. Cole's candidacy has been rather **tepid**. The party needs a more vigorous show of enthusiasm if he is to be the nominee.*

- *"Your looks are okay,"* was Stanley Kowalski's rather **tepid** endorsement of Blanche Dubois's need for confirmation of her appeal.

4 funny words

Alfalfa—a kind of hay crop—is a word that just sounds funny. But we're talking here about words that describe types of funniness or results of funniness. Some of these are fairly common, but we bet you'll find some that will be new friends.

1. Risible (RIZ-uh-bull)

This word meaning "relating to laughter" can describe a person who is feeling inclined to laugh, but it is more frequently used to describe remarks or situations that are likely to provoke laughter. Coming from the Latin for "laugh," this word is the cheery relative of *derisive*, which means "laughing at in the sense of mocking or jeering." The not very common noun form is **risibility**.

- *On another night Niko would probably have laughed at the stand-up comedian's jokes, but he was not in a very **risible** mood the day he learned about his low grade in physics.*

- *The cartoonish stereotype of a **risible** situation is that of a man in a top hat slipping on a banana.*

2. Rabelaisian (rab-a-LAZE-ee-un)

This adjective refers to satirical humor of a broad and earthy variety. The word comes from the name of a hilarious sixteenth-century French writer, François Rabelais. The word is usually capitalized, further accentuating its connection with the author.

- *Morgan thought the short story was hilarious and, with the important exception of its **Rabelaisian** humor, the kind of thing he'd like to teach his eighth-grade class.*

- *Plans for Dana's bachelor party involved gift ideas of a fairly **Rabelaisian** nature.*

3. Sardonic (sar-DON-ik)

This adjective refers to a humor that is cynical or scornfully mocking. Some historians of language think it derives from a kind of humor attributed to natives of the Mediterranean island of Sardinia.

- *Although the play Hamlet is officially a tragedy, there is much humor in it, especially in the **sardonic** wit of the title character.*

- *"If you keep lowering my salary, I'll have to tighten my belt a lot," said Greg. "Or eat the belt itself," he added **sardonically**.*

4. Buffoon (buff-OON)

A person who enjoys clowning or joking around, or one whose normal behavior is perceived as ridiculous. This noun comes from the Italian word *buffa* meaning "jest." (A comic opera is, even in English, referred to as an *opera buffa*.)

- *J. D. enjoyed playing the **buffoon** in study hall, mimicking Ms. Springer's facial expressions behind her back, then feigning total innocence as she turned to glare at him.*

- *Tony thinks his antics are original and witty, but most people regard him as a complete **buffoon**.*

5. Cachinnation (KACK-a-nay-shun)

This scholarly noun refers to a loud or convulsive kind of laughter. It may not derive from the same root as *cackle*, but associating the two will help you remember it.

- *The governess could at times hear strange **cachinnations** from the attic, and she wondered what servant could be there and why the servant would be laughing so harshly.*

- *Hermione's remark was so offensive that Myrtle could not decide whether to strike her or merely to **cachinnate** in a slow, derisive manner.*

*The French **farce** featured three swinging doors, a trapdoor, and four windows: characters repeatedly missed each other by seconds, causing the audience to roar with laughter each time it happened.*

6. Caricature (KARE-a-ka-ture or -chure)

Whether it's used as a verb or a noun, *caricature* refers to satiric humor, good-natured or cruel, that exaggerates or distorts in words or images one feature of the object of the attack.

- *Philip Guston's paintings attacking Richard Nixon transcend the usual **caricature** of the man.*

- *When Rachel was ill at ease, she sometimes found it helpful to find a way to **caricature** her own discomfort and, by this mockery, diminish its force.*

7. Farce (farse)

A farce is a comic play characterized by improbable but humorous elements. By extension, the word can describe anything so absurd as to be laughable, whether by its humor or the fact that it makes a mockery, a joke, of an undertaking. (And isn't it a little bit funny that the origin of this word means "seasoned stuffing"?) The adjective form is **farcical**.

- *The French **farce** featured three swinging doors, a trapdoor, and four windows: characters repeatedly missed each other by seconds, causing the audience to roar with laughter each time it happened.*

- *"Student government at Montrose High is **farcical**," complained Annemarie. "Kids just run for office so they can list it on their college applications."*

8. Antics (AN-ticks)

This noun describes acts that are perceived as either

amusing or not at all amusing, depending on the context or on the personality of the beholder. Strangely enough, it derives from the same root word as *antique*, although modern uses have no hint of age about them.

- *The **antics** of the trained dog wearing a tutu had even the most sophisticated audience member hee-hawing.*

- *Ms. Ford has just about had it with the **antics** of her last period class: is signing a classmate's yearbook really more important than passing the algebra exam?*

9. Droll (rhymes with *hole*)

This adjective describes words, facial expressions, or acts that are amusing in an odd way, perhaps somewhat whimsical. The fact that it comes from a medieval English word for "goblin" may help us sense its flavor.

- *The audience responded very favorably to Louis's **droll** presentation of Puck; at first they weren't sure whether to laugh or not.*

- *The **droll** look on Jeff Foxworthy's face made his supporters laugh even before he began his comic routine.*

10. Lampoon (lam-POON)

Supposedly, this word has its origin as a refrain word in German drinking songs. This is appropriate background information for this noun or verb that refers to ridiculing or mocking someone or something. As with much satire, its tone can range from lighthearted to cruel.

- *The* magazine *National* **Lampoon** *lives up to its name in its free-ranging attacks on customs and politics.*

- *After Gregor lost the hot-dog-eating contest by half a wiener,* **lampoons** *of his defeat appeared all over campus with the mocking slogan "Half a Frank Short!"*

5 farrago

A farrago (fur-RAH-go) is a hodgepodge, a mixture, a conglomeration. And that's what you have here—an admixture of varied terms, with a medley of mixed meanings. Every five chapters you'll come across a collection of this nature.

1. Libretto (luh-BRET-toe)

The musical notations of an opera or other extended musical composition are collectively known as the score. The words to be sung (or the written text of these words) are called the libretto. The word's literal meaning is "little book." One who writes a libretto is referred to as a **librettist**.

- *The soprano said that although the baritone was very familiar with the* **libretto,** *she didn't believe he knew the score.*

- *Is it fair that Giuseppe Verdi gets all the praise for the opera* Otello *while his* **librettist** *Arrigo Boito goes almost unmentioned?*

2. Pubescent (pyoo-BESS-ent)

This adjective means "having reached puberty or the stage of adolescence in which an individual becomes capable of sexual reproduction." It also means "covered with short hairs or soft down"—perhaps a description of the cheek of a pubescent boy? The noun is **pubescence** or **puberty**.

- *"You're acting like a **pubescent** girl," Clothilde's fiancé insisted. "We're planning an engagement party, not a Bat Mitzvah."*

- *Sandy could tell by the braces, the pimples, and the budding mustache that Zachary had reached **pubescence**; she hoped he would now finally ask her to go on a date instead of playing "Cowboys and Indians" in his backyard.*

3. Anomie (AN-oh-mee)

The original French meaning of this noun is "lawlessness," but it has taken on a more complex social and philosophical meaning. When one suffers anomie, one has a feeling of alienation and purposelessness caused by a lack of standards, values, and ideals.

- *His silent friend wandered away in solitude and **anomie**.*

- *The dark, brooding student, lost in his thoughts, could not conceal his **anomie**.*

4. Quantum (KWAN-tum)

You know already, don't you, that a "quantum leap" is a common phrase for a big change. But you may also enjoy knowing this is one of those intriguing linguistic incidences where popular use of a word changes its meaning. *Quantum*, as a physics term, refers to the *smallest* possible change that can be measured. One scientist cleverly describes it as "such an infinitesimal level as to be infinite." Before it became wedded to *leap*, *quantum* was simply the Latin word for "quantity," and you'll occasionally see it in older writing.

- *Eighteenth-century writer Tobias Smollett describes himself as having "a respectable **quantum** of knowledge."*

- *What Shakespeare expressed as "a sea change" in his play* The Tempest *is now, in our scientific age, more often termed a **quantum** leap.*

5. Quidnunc (KWID-nunk)

Here's another term that you'll find useful now and then. The origin (it's from the Latin for "what now?") gives us a broad hint that this noun refers to a nosy person, a busybody, someone always eager to hear and spread gossip.

- *Uh-oh, here comes Quentin the **quidnunc**—don't tell him a word of what I said, or he'll have it all over town by sundown.*

- *Great minds focus on things like vocabulary improvement; **quidnuncs** are concerned with people (and especially their private lives).*

*"I do not like **polygamy** or even moderate **bigamy**," sings the Welsh governess in the musical* The King and I. *"I realize that in your eyes that clearly makes a prig of me."*

6. Assiduous (uh-SID-you-us)

This adjective suggests diligence, persistence. Unsurprisingly (or maybe not), it comes from the Latin for "to sit," implying the ability to stay in your seat until the job's done.

- *Yurah was so **assiduous** in her work on the Intel grant project that her parents had to remind her of the importance of food and sleep.*

- *"**Assiduous** I'm not," bragged Bo, whose work was frequently shown in Outsider Art Fairs. "But still I manage to get stuff done and people like it."*

7. Ersatz (ER-zots or ER-zats)

This German immigrant means "imitation, substitute, replacement." Note that its use strongly suggests inferiority or lower quality. You wouldn't likely refer to a higher-performing athlete (maybe a pinch-hitter) as ersatz, but you might well use the term for something made of cheaper materials.

- *The thief may have thought he'd made a big haul, but the jewels he took were paste—purely **ersatz**.*

- *The hoaxer tried to pass his paintings off as Picassos, but the curator immediately recognized them as **ersatz**.*

8. Incubus (IN-kyoo-bus)

In medieval folklore, this malevolent demon could sexually attack women in their sleep. Now time has transformed that frightening image into any oppressive burden that torments an individual as a nightmare might torment. And indeed the word derives from the Latin word for "nightmare."

- *After the Civil War there was much rejoicing that America had at last freed itself from the **incubus** of slavery.*

- *My twenty-page term paper on endangered species oppressed me all semester. I'm glad to be free of that **incubus**.*

9. Imbroglio (im-BROL-lee-yo)

This noun comes to us straight from the Italian word for "tangle." It means "a confused or complicated disagreement" or, quite simply, "an entanglement." You might use it to describe a small battle such as a fare dispute with a taxi driver, or a larger argument with complicated international implications.

- *What an evening! Hernando accidentally left his wallet in the taxi, we arrived late at the theatre, and we got into quite an **imbroglio** with the box office manager over his letting us in without our tickets.*

- *The political **imbroglio** surrounding the controversy over same-sex marriage will most likely remain a strong issue in future presidential races.*

10. Polygamy (puh-LIG-a-mee)

Made up of the root words for "many" and "marriage," this word refers to having more than one spouse—particularly to having more than two. (The legal term **bigamy** is most often used when one person is wed to two others.) If we change the root word for "marriage" to the root for "man" (*andro*) or "woman," (*gyn*), we get more specialized terms such as **polyandry** (pol-ee-AND-ree) and **polygyny** (puh-LIJ-uh-nee), meaning having more than one husband or more than one wife.

- *"I do not like **polygamy** or even moderate **bigamy**," sings the Welsh governess in the musical* The King and I. *"I realize that in your eyes that clearly makes a prig of me."*

- *The cult-leading preacher insisted that he had married the six young women because his religion considered **polygyny** the ideal marital arrangement.*

Quiz #1

CATEGORY A

Match each definition on the right with the appropriate word in the column on the left.

_____ animus   A. amusing

_____ disparage   B. lack of energy

_____ droll   C. feeling of dislike

_____ ersatz   D. to put down

_____ inertia   E. imitation

CATEGORY B

Select a word from the list below that best fits each of the sentences on the next page. Some words won't be used at all.

anomie	ennui
incubus	lacerated
libretto	pubescent
temerity	truculent

1. I can't believe that you had the _____ to challenge the speaker on facts within her area of expertise.

2. I wasn't really bored; I just felt I didn't belong there. I had a sense of _____.

3. He couldn't believe she was so enraged at him. She verbally _____ him.

4. Nick is getting really handsome as he enters his _____ years and is losing his baby fat.

5. I'd prefer that you got angry at me rather than being so _____; grumbling and sullenness do not become you.

CATEGORY C

1. You meet a feckless jingoist. What's this person like?

2. He specializes in scathing sardonic criticism. Do you find his criticism helpful? Why or why not?

3. She went into a diatribe about recent events, excoriating her colleagues. How pleasant was this to listen to?

4. Does a sense of lassitude seem likely in bellicose times? Explain.

5. Maybe some day I'll see it as farcical, but right now this imbroglio is making me feel fractious. Explain.

6 lighthearted words

Many of these words suggest happiness, a carefree mood, or perhaps an unexpected bit of sparkle or style. The final entry brings in, for balance, the complementary negative aspect of lightheartedness.

1. Élan (ay-LAN)

This noun comes from the Old French word for "rush," originally from the Latin for "to throw a lance." Like *brio* (see #3), it means "enthusiastic liveliness," but it can also be used, like *panache* (see #5), to mean "a dash of style."

- *With his bright yellow scarf and beret, Pierre's **élan** was obvious to everyone at the biology fair; it was clear he was no ordinary scientist.*

- *Although she was the only woman to wear her Easter bonnet to the postparade luncheon, Gladys dressed with so much **élan** that the hat seemed perfectly appropriate.*

2. Cachet (cash-AY)

This noun originally meant "a seal affixed to a letter or document to mark its authenticity," but it has since come to mean "a mark of quality or a distinguishing feature." It comes from the Old French word for "to press."

- *The nosegay he wore in his buttonhole gave* ***cachet*** *to Mr. Giovanelli's otherwise unremarkable blue suit.*

- *Lots of teenagers like to buy clothing with a designer label prominently displayed because they think it gives* ***cachet*** *to their outfits.*

3. Brio (BREE-oh)

From the Italian word for "fire" or "life," this noun means "vivacity" or "spirit." It is generally used to describe a way of doing something. It may have entered the English language from the musical instruction "con brio," which means "with energy."

- *"Let's go, everybody!" Dan shouted with* ***brio*** *as he led the tired scouts up the mountain. "We can make it!"*

- *The performer recited Homer's* Odyssey *with* ***brio***, *galvanizing the students with his engaging recounting of Odysseus's struggle with the Sirens.*

4. Éclat (ay-KLAH)

This French noun has come straight into English to describe a brilliant performance or the appreciation such a performance might receive. Rhymes with "Hey-Pa."

- *Dressed in a purple robe tipped with ermine, Prince Boyohboy entered the kingdom with great **éclat**.*

- *When the company gave the name **Éclat** to one model of its luxury cars, it probably hoped to evoke a sense of both sterling performance and admiration.*

5. Panache (pan-OSH or pan-ASH)

From the Latin word that means "plume," this noun means a touch of added style or dash. Just picture a brilliantly colored feather emerging from a Roman helmet, and you'll get the idea.

- *Jeanette decided to tie a crimson scarf around her neck to add **panache** to her otherwise dull gray business suit.*

- *"The rhinestone buttons add **panache** to this wool coat," said the salesgirl at the chic boutique. "You'll wow them on opening night."*

*To be true to the spirit of a **lagniappe,** this entry in the vocabulary book should have been an eleventh entry in the chapter, an extra, above and beyond what's expected.*

6. Insouciant (in-SOO-see-ont)

Coming from the Old French word for "not troubled," this adjective means "nonchalant, coolly unconcerned, or blithely indifferent." The noun form is **insouciance**.

- *Mrs. Winthrop walked her dog Bubbles with her usual **insouciance**, allowing him to jump on strangers and trample the gardens of her neighbors.*

- *I had mixed feeling about his **insouciant** expression after hearing the devastating news about the colleague he disliked.*

7. Coruscate (KOR-us-cate)

This verb comes from the Latin word meaning "to sparkle" and can be used either literally or figuratively. The noun form is **coruscating**.

- *The film made sharp visual contrast between the life of poor Russian women in drab shawls and the luxury at the czar's ball, where figures in shimmering taffeta wore **coruscating** diamonds, emeralds, and sapphires.*

- *Prof. McIntosh sets high standards for students in his classes, but they continue to sign up because his **coruscating** wit makes his lectures a delight.*

8. Panoply (PAN-uh-plee)

This noun is used for a striking or splendid display, often in association with events such as a coronation or a state funeral. It originally denoted a full suit of armor, which must, in its fully polished condition, have given off quite a sheen.

- *When Doreen first visited the United Nations, she was delighted by the **panoply** of flags of all the countries represented there.*

- *The **panoply** of Pope John Paul II's funeral fascinated even viewers who had no religious associations with the ceremony.*

9. Lagniappe (LAN-yap)

This noun first referred to a small gift a store owner might give a customer, but is coming increasingly to be used as "an unexpected extra gift or benefit." With roots in New World Spanish and Quechua, it was originally used in the Creole dialect of Louisiana.

- *Customers gave Bolling's Department Store a lot of repeat business because their children enjoyed the lollipops Mr. Bolling gave them as a **lagniappe**.*

- *To be true to the spirit of a **lagniappe**, this entry in the vocabulary book should have been an eleventh entry in the chapter, an extra, above and beyond what's expected.*

10. Cavalier (cav-uh-LEER)

This adjective now almost always has the negative sense of an offhand or disdainful dismissal of an important topic. It's a good example of a word moving from positive to negative, for it once expressed the jaunty concept of a carefree spirit or the gallantry of a knight. (The noun *cavalier* originally contained the aristocratic idea of a man wealthy enough to own a horse.)

- *The fact that Mr. Malcolm, the CEO, is himself wealthy does not give him the right to have a **cavalier** attitude toward affordable health insurance for his employees.*

- *When Hamlet says that he once considered good handwriting a mark of "baseness," is he expressing a **cavalier** contempt for qualities that might be important to wage-earners?*

7 logophile words

This book offers you twenty-four chapters of words that are selected for their usefulness in your reading, your writing, and your speech. Here's the exception: ten words that are, paradoxically, of limited practical use. Maybe they'll be of great curiosity value as you amaze your friends with remarks such as "Did you know there's a word for the little mark that shows where to start a new paragraph?" We like these words, but then we're logophiles (lovers of words), and we enjoy trying to persuade others to join our ranks.

1. Pilcrow (PIL-crow)

Yes, there is indeed a name for that mark you might handwrite on a manuscript to show where a new paragraph starts. Where it comes from is uncertain, but most experts speculate that it's a very corrupted form of the word *paragraph* itself.

- *The top of the **pilcrow** may look like a backwards "P," but it's really a "C"—the "C" stands for the Latin word "capitulum," meaning chapter or division.*

- *Did Adam Mars-Jones title his novel **Pilcrow** in order to send an early signal of the main character's interest in language?*

2. Borborygmus (bor-bor-IG-mus)

You could just say, "Your stomach's growling," but wouldn't it sound more impressive to say "I note you are having an episode of borborygmus"? This word for that intestinal noise comes from the Greek for "rumbling" and sounds like what it means.

- *The embarrassment caused by his severe and frequent bouts of **borborygmus** prompted him to ask a doctor if there might be a medical remedy.*

- *A poem by Vladimir Nabokov refers to the noises of a mid-twentieth-century refrigerator as **borborgymus**.*

3. Funambulist (fyoo-NAM-byoo-list)

This comes straight from the Latin word meaning "tightrope walker." (Yes, the Romans had them too.)

- *The most famous **funambulist** is probably Philippe Petit, who walked a rope between the two towers of the World Trade Center in 1974.*

- *Squirrels are so proficient at walking on branches and clotheslines that we might consider them the **funambulists** of the animal world.*

4. Struthious (STROO-thee-us)

This interesting adjective means "referring to ostriches" and comes directly from the Latin word for that creature.

Everybody knows *canine* and *feline*, but this animal word definitely falls in the "Did you know that...?" category.

- *I almost bought the wallet with the embossed crocodile print, but in the end I chose the less familiar* **struthious** *pattern.*

- *His psychologist is helping him learn to confront his problems rather than to engage in the* **struthious** *behavior of sticking his head in the sand.*

5. Callipygian (cal-a-PIJ-yun)

Yes, there's an elegant adjective from classical Greek that means "having beautiful buttocks."

- *The ancient marble statues had many examples, Lester noted, of* **callipygian** *males and females.*

- *The erudite cartoon depicted a construction worker who was watching a shapely woman stroll by as saying, "Wow! Dig that* **callipygian** *babe!"*

There is, perhaps, a gray area between the commendable goal of wanting all details of a project to be exactly right and being a loathsome **doryphore**.

6. Doryphore (DOR-a-fore)

This word may actually prove useful. It was coined by Harold Nicholson in the 1940s to refer to a person who takes delight in pointing out the small mistakes of others. Its syllables come from the Greek words for "spear carrier," possibly with the idea that the doryphore uses a figurative laser pointer to call attention to your errors.

- *"Don't be such a **doryphore**, John! No one else in this office cares that the handout I distributed is printed on paper that has the watermark upside down."*

- *There is, perhaps, a gray area between the commendable goal of wanting all details of a project to be exactly right and being a loathsome **doryphore**.*

7. Omphaloskeptic (om-FAL-o-skep-tic)

Do you get your best ideas through prolonged solitary meditation? Why, then, you may belong to the ranks of the omphaloskeptics: those who engage in contemplative gazing at their own respective navels. Needless to say, it's often used humorously.

- *Spending time alone and forming your own opinions is important, but if you never exchange ideas with others you may fall into unhealthy **omphaloskepticism**.*

- *"I'm burned out," said Marina. "I need to get away from work and spend a little time as a hammock-lying **omphaloskeptic**."*

8. Noyade (nwa-YAHD)

This French word refers to mass drowning, particularly as a form of execution. It would be easier to take pleasure in this curious word if it did not refer to historical fact during the Reign of Terror that followed the French Revolution.

- *Chapter 12 of the French history book gave upsetting details of the **noyade** in the town of Nantes, where many priests were taken out in a boat and drowned in midstream.*

- *"Let's have several lifeguards on duty. This event is supposed to help us bond as a group, and a **noyade** would not accomplish our goal," noted the official in charge of planning the office beach party.*

9. Defenestration (de-fen-es-TRAY-shun)

Here's another odd word for a strange punishment, one that also has historical precedent. It literally refers to being thrown out a window, an event that obviously has the potential to cause great harm or death.

- *Although there was an earlier precedent, the term "the **Defenestration** of Prague" usually refers to an event in the seventeenth century when religious protestors were tossed out a castle window. Happily, they survived.*

- *After mischievous young Georgy tossed many toys out the window of his second-floor playroom, his mother had to assign a penalty for deliberate **defenestration**.*

10. Ucalegon (u-KAL-uh-gon)

You won't find it in every dictionary, but the idea of a word that means "a neighbor whose house is on fire" is too good to omit. Its scholarly origins are in Homer and Virgil, where a neighbor of Aeneas named Ucalegon loses his house to fire. (Literally, the Greek roots of *ucalegon* mean something like "What, me worry?")

- *The Roman satirist Juvenal depicts **Ucalegon**, a man trying desperately to move his possessions out of a firetrap apartment of the sort so common in ancient Rome.*

- *"Would **Ucalegon** be a good or a bad name for a company selling fire insurance?" queried Marcy, our scholarly colleague.*

8 mental words

Your thoughts, your knowledge, your judgment, your memory—they're all up there in your brain. These ten words refer to different aspects of those mighty lobes.

1. Mnemonic (ni-MON-ic)

This adjective refers to memory or relating to memory. (And do remember the *m* is silent.) You'll most often see or hear this word in the phrase *mnemonic device*. The noun **mnemonics** refers to memory in general. If your fifth-grade teacher gave you the word *HOMES* to help you remember the Great Lakes, then you've used a mnemonic device. Mnemosyne was the Greek goddess of memory—and here's a mnemonic device to remember that fact. She was the mother of nine daughters, many of whom had four-syllable names such as Terpsichore, and so she had to be the goddess of memory to remember them all.

- *I find **mnemonics** fascinating: why can I sometimes remember that a person's name starts with an "S," but I can't remember the name?*

- *Ms. Bevilacqua loves **mnemonic** devices: she taught her seventh graders to spell "rhythm" correctly by having them chant, "Ride Hard, You Thick-Headed Monster."*

2. Didactic (dye-DAK-tik)

From the Greek word for "taught," this adjective means "intended to instruct." It is sometimes used negatively to describe someone who teaches or moralizes excessively. **Didact** is the noun form.

- *Though the minister often gave interesting sermons during weekly chapel, he had a tendency to be too **didactic**.*

- *Sometimes the best-educated people are the ones who consider themselves **autodidacts**; lack of a formal education does not mean someone is unintelligent.*

3. Erudite (ERR-yeh-dite)

This adjective has an interesting history. It comes from the Latin roots for "untaught" or "rude." In English, however, it was used to mean "learned" as early as the fifteenth century and, though it was used only sarcastically for periods of time, it was ultimately used only to mean "learned" or "scholarly." The noun form is **erudition**.

- *The students at State College love Professor Krupotkin because he is generous with his time, creative in his teaching methods, and so **erudite** in the field of Russian history.*

- *Isabella's **erudition** became quite obvious during her lecture at the Archeological Institute; she has translated more than twenty-five languages, including Sanskrit, Mandarin, and ancient Greek.*

4. Judicious (joo-DISH-us)

If you're judicious, you exercise good judgment; you're prudent. You'll hear the echo in *judicial,* which refers to the system of courts and official judges, but you can be judicious even when you're far away from a courtroom.

- *"No, Bryn," said Mr. Brummel to his fourteen-year-old daughter, "you may not have an iguana tattooed onto your wrist. Such a decision would not be **judicious**."*

- ***Judiciously**, Martin packed an extra supply of batteries, even though his hiking trip was to be a short one.*

5. Immemorial (im-meh-MOR-ee-ul)

This adjective refers to things whose existence, literally or figuratively, outlives memory.

- *One book on the problems in the Middle East is titled* Time ***Immemorial**, suggesting conflict in that region has existed for a very long time.*

- *One fascinating aspect of geology is that rocks of **immemorial** age have stories to tell to those who know how to interpret their appearance.*

*Hamlet rather extravagantly promises the ghost of his father that he'll **obliterate** all thoughts from his brain except for the command to avenge his father's murder.*

6. Polymath (POL-ee-math)

A polymath is someone who really knows a lot, in many different fields. *Poly-* means "many," and the root of *math* is "knowledge," and when you put them together, that's what you get.

- *While Walter's profession is medicine, he's a real **polymath**, someone who enjoys conversations about art, music, law, and kayaking.*

- *"I don't aspire to be a **polymath**," said Joelle, "but I hope to be well-educated enough to understand news stories about both science and the humanities."*

7. Obliterate (ob-LIT-er-ate)

If you obliterate something, it's as if you wipe out all memory of it.

- *The powerfully satiric movie* Dr. Strangelove *deals with the possibility of warring nations with nuclear bombs **obliterating** life on earth.*

- *Hamlet rather extravagantly promises the ghost of his father that he'll **obliterate** all thoughts from his* *brain except for the command to avenge his father's murder.*

8. Empirical (em-PEER-ik-al)

This is an adjective about learning, not teaching. A student who learns empirically is "guided by practical experience or observation rather than by precepts or theory." It comes from the Greek word for "experienced." The noun form is **empiric**.

- *Andrew noted that the man seemed to be exhibiting the textbook definitions of psychotic behavior, but **empirical** evidence suggested that anxiety, not psychosis, was the cause.*

- *The university president was shunned by the public for insisting that women are weaker in math and science than men, without any real academic basis or **empirical** proof for his assumptions.*

9. Obfuscate (OB-fuss-kate)

This verb comes from the Latin for "to darken over" and means to make something confusing or difficult to understand. One often obfuscates intentionally in order to hide the truth. The noun is **obfuscation**.

- *"Do not **obfuscate** the truth," Mr. Gekko's lawyer advised him. "The jury will know when you are trying to cover up your intentions."*

- *When Sam's mother asked him where he was going so late at night, his answer was so full of **obfuscation** that she was sure he was up to no good.*

10. Ratiocination (rashy-ossa-NAY-shun)

This is the process of using a logical, carefully reasoned thinking process. (Think of the adjective *rational*.) And it's such a satisfying six-syllable word to say. The verb form is **ratiocinate**.

- *Edgar Allan Poe specialized in tales of **ratiocination**; one example is his famous story "The Gold Bug," in which a cryptic message has to be deciphered.*

- *Some scientists reach their discoveries through sudden bursts of revelation; others do so through step-by-step **ratiocination**.*

9 nature words

The following words about nature can be useful, whether you're talking about the wave of rocks and dirt a glacier pushes in front of it (*moraine*), or about a friend who explores caves (*spelunker* or *speleologist*). And as a bonus, you can use many of these words metaphorically, as when you're physically or intellectually in unknown territory (*terra incognita*).

1. Arboreal (are-BOR-ree-ul)

This word can mean "resembling a tree or trees" or "living in trees." It comes from the Latin *arbor,* meaning "tree."

- *Arboreal monkeys probably adapted themselves to tree-living to avoid predators.*

- *The construction cranes gave an arboreal aspect to the skyline.*

2. Riparian (ruh-PAIR-ee-un)

Waterfront property is usually valuable, and was perhaps even more so to ancient tribes who subsisted on fish, shellfish, and other fruits of rivers and lakes. *Riparian* is a somewhat general term that means "having to do with the banks of a river or other body of water."

- *Everyone who lives on the shore has **riparian** rights to the water.*

- *The summer residents built sturdy and attractive **riparian** cottages.*

3. Terra incognita (TER-uh in-cog-NEAT-uh)

Literally meaning "unknown territory," this term can be used for physical territory or for any situation in which you find yourself on new or unfamiliar figurative ground.

- *The photography show, titled **Terra Incognita**, included amazing photographs of Antarctica.*

- *Pulitzer-Prize winner E. O. Wilson says that much of the world at our feet, and even inside our bodies, is **terra incognita**.*

4. Limnology (lim-NOL-la-gee)

Given that water is so important to us, and that we love living near it, we're not surprised that there's a branch of scientific study devoted to lakes, ponds, and other freshwater resources. One who studies limnology is a **limnologist**.

- *If John Steinbeck's character had lived farther inland, he would have been a **limnologist** instead of a marine biologist.*

- *The lecturing **limnologist** amazed us with slides about the many species of aquatic life in our nearby lakes and ponds.*

5. Eutrophication (you-tru-fuh-KAY-shun)

We're still on the subject of lakes, here, but with an unusual and interesting word. The prefix *eu-* means "good," so you'd expect something pleasant to be going on. And it is—for aquatic weeds and algae. But unfortunately, it's bad news for the lake. Eutrophication can be caused by runoff of minerals and fertilizer, and results in an abundant increase in the accumulation of algae and other organisms that deplete the oxygen and destroy marine life. The adjective form is **eutrophying**.

- *The engineers waxed enthusiastic about the benefits of the proposed dam, never mentioning the inevitable **eutrophication** that the limnologists had said was sure to result.*

- *Many of the "beneficial" ideas proposed to help our society turn out to have **eutrophying** effects— some improvement in one area but with wider negative effects.*

*Pulitzer-Prize winner E. O. Wilson says that much of the world at our feet, and even inside our bodies, is **terra incognita**.*

6. Speleology (spee-lee-OL-la-gee)

Caves, like most features of nature, have their own cadre of scientists who study them. These scientists are **speleologists**, from the Latin term for "cave." (If you explore caves as a hobby, you're a **spelunker**.)

- *How strange that Kryptak, who was a bit claustrophobic, should become a **speleologist**.*

- *I might have gone into **speleology**, but I could never remember the difference between stalactites and stalagmites.*

7. Loam (rhymes with *home*)

An earthy little word, loam is the name given to some of the most-fertile soil—rich, tillable stuff that usually contains at least a little sand and silt, and maybe some clay. The adjective form is **loamy**.

- *The early explorers found lowland valleys covered with deep layers of rich, **loamy** soil.*

- *During the dust-bowl days, relentless winds stripped the **loam** from the land, leaving it barren and sterile.*

8. Moraine (mor-RAIN)

A moraine is the accumulated debris (boulders, gravel, and such) carried along and deposited by a glacier.

- *The extensive **moraine** clearly showed where the glacier had stopped.*

- *A **moraine** in Spain would be a pain.*

9. Delta (DELL-tuh)

Many of our interesting words come from Greek—as does this one. But *delta* is different from most in that it comes from one specific uppercase letter of the Greek alphabet: it's the shape of the letter Δ (delta) that makes it an appropriate name for the triangle-shape of the mouth of a river.

- *Few people think of the Mississippi **delta** as being a triangular soil deposit; they're more likely to associate it with the soulful music called the blues.*

- *From the airplane window, I could clearly see the **delta** where the river flowed into the gulf.*

10. Tectonics (tek-TON-ics)

This word can mean "the science of architecture and construction," but when applied to study of the earth, it means "the branch of geology dealing with the earth's crust, especially its faulting and folding."

- *The **tectonic** plates in the earth's crust may jam against each other—and when they suddenly slip, we have an earthquake.*

- *Some scientists who study **tectonics** say that our earth's visible surface originally consisted of one giant continent—Pangaea (pan-JEE-uh).*

10. gallimaufry

The word *gallimaufry* (pronounced gal-la-MAW-free) comes from an Old French word for "stew or mixture." And that's what you have here—a mixture, jumble, assorted group of odds and ends—the second chapter of this variety.

1. Pulchritude (PULK-ruh-tyood or -tood)

Here's a noun that sounds ugly but means great beauty. The adjective form is **pulchritudinous**.

- *Helen of Troy's face was renowned for its **pulchritude**.*

- *The soldiers in the trench were overwhelmed by the **pulchritude** of the sunset.*

2. Vade mecum (VAH-dee MAY-kum)

The Latin meaning of this term is "go with me," which suggests its modern meaning. Your vade mecum is something (often a book or manual) that you almost always carry with you for frequent use or ready reference.

- *That girl is a true onomatomaniac—her dictionary is her **vade mecum**.*

- *Here comes the ornithologist, his bird-guide **vade mecum** under his arm as always.*

3. Hoary (HOR-ee)

Someone who is hoary is not full of hair (*hirsute*)—unless it is gray hair. The adjective means "gray- or white-haired" and implies advanced age. The white-haired, white-bearded seaman in Samuel Taylor Coleridge's poem "The Rime of the Ancient Mariner" is described as hoary.

- *The chestnut-colored hair of Vladimir's youth had paled and turned **hoary** with age.*

- *I can't believe Igor expected me to laugh at his **hoary** joke; I first heard it when I was ten years old.*

4. Skein (skane)

Granted, you won't need this word often. But when you want a word to tell about a twisted coil (of yarn, string, or such), this is the one for you. It also has another meaning—a lined-up flock of birds in flight.

- *Her **skein** of loosely braided hair hung comfortably at the back of her neck.*

- *Geese on the ground form a gaggle; in flight, they're a **skein**.*

5. Nuance (NOO-aunce)

This noun refers to subtle or slight variation and to sensitivity to those variations. An awareness of nuance is important on the social scene as well as in areas of greater import. (*Nuance* is derived from the Latin word for that changeable phenomenon, the cloud.)

- *Mrs. Ramsay's awareness of the finely layered **nuances** in her guests' interactions was comparable to an orchestra conductor's awareness of the balance among instruments.*

- *Prof. Duffy is so sensitive to **nuances** in poetic style that he can often guess the author of poems he has not previously read.*

*Some see Hamlet as **querulous**, but most Shakespeare lovers would claim that the beauty of his language and his wit redeem him.*

6. Concomitant (con-COM-mit-unt)

Something that's concomitant occurs or exists concurrently with something else, often in a subordinate or resulting sense.

- *As usual, he rushed to judgment; as usual, the result was a skein of **concomitant** problems.*

- *The new process not only increased production, it produced a **concomitant** increase in profits.*

7. Restive (RES-tiv)

Though it sounds like *restless,* this adjective means something slightly different. It comes from the Old French *rester,* meaning "to remain," and it means "to resist control or be impatient under restriction." It's not quite audacity but it does suggest a bold resistance to rule.

- *The students grew restive under the watchful eyes of the principal and began thinking of ways to avoid detention.*

- *The government did nothing to reduce casualties during the war, and the rebellious students grew more and more restive during their demonstrations.*

8. Pillory (PILL-er-ee)

This is the name for those old wooden frameworks with holes for the head, hands, and feet of offenders who were to be put on public display. Now most commonly a verb, it means "to expose someone to public shame and derision."

- *Some of the media gave her praise and plaudits, while others pilloried her unmercifully.*

- *The prosecuting attorney's opening statement was so trenchant that it seemed his goal was to pillory the defendant.*

9. Querulous (KWER-u-lus)

This adjective comes from the same Latin root as *quarrel,* but instead of arguing, the querulous person whines, complains, and grumbles.

- *Until you've spent your birthday taking care of a pair of **querulous** toddlers, you don't know the full beauty of a few moments of solitude.*

- *Some see Hamlet as **querulous,** but most Shakespeare lovers would claim that the beauty of his language and his wit redeem him.*

10. Mountebank (MOUNT-uh-bank)

Examples of this particular type of clown are largely found in accounts of earlier eras: they told stories and jokes, and even did some magic tricks in order to attract a crowd of folks to whom they could attempt to sell ineffective medicines. The history of the word—Italian for "jump up on the bench"—allows us to visualize the start of their crowd-gathering tactics. Today the word might be used for any unscrupulous salesperson, whether joke-telling or not.

- *Perhaps Michiko is romanticizing the past when she says she finds the nerve and skill of marketplace **mountebanks** somewhat appealing.*

- *That used car salesman turned out to be a bit of a **mountebank;** his dashing flattery disguised the fact that the car was a lemon.*

Quiz #2

Match each definition on the right with the appropriate word in the column on the left.

_____ concomitant   A. relating to or assisting memory

_____ hoary   B. white or white-haired with age

_____ mnemonic   C. relating to banks of a river

_____ obliterate   D. going along with, occurring at the same time

_____ riparian   E. to strike out all traces of

CATEGORY B

Select a word from the list below that best fits each of the sentences on the next page. Some words won't be used at all.

brio	callipygian
didactic	funambulist
lagniappe	mountebank
obfuscation	tectonics

1. Your collection of _____ statuary is intriguing—such a specialized interest!

2. If you don't want to confuse me, I trust you will eschew _____.

3. The orchestra really got into the happy mood of the Rossini overture and played it with _____.

4. So Laertes bought that poison from a _____? Can we be sure it will work?

5. His _____ manner can sometimes be off-putting, but he's really interested in making sure all his students do well on the final.

CATEGORY C

1. You say your attitude toward the matter is judicious; I say it's cavalier. Explain the nature of this disagreement.

2. Although he's very erudite, he's also perceptive, understanding every nuance of social situations. Explain.

3. Your punishment will be placement in the pillory or a command to listen to a recording of several hours of borborygmus. Which do you choose and why?

4. That doryphore just places too much emphasis on ratiocination. Explain.

5. You're in an arboreal setting. Do you choose to be joined by a polymath or someone insouciant? How do you decide?

11

"no" words

You can say "no" to a drink, to the right to vote, to bawdy language, to progress, to punishment. Some of these ten words are words of denial; others indicate some other variety of negation.

1. Abstemious (ab-STEEM-e-us)

While its literal meaning can refer to moderate eating and drinking, it's often associated with not drinking alcoholic beverages—perhaps because its sound is similar to *abstinence* (from the verb *abstain*). A related word for one who partakes of no alcoholic beverages is **teetotaler**, coined by the nineteenth-century Temperance movement. However, abstemious is often used now to describe abstaining from premarital sex.

- *Accustomed to what he termed "the good life," Smithers found prolonged visits with more **abstemious** relatives not only unpleasant but painful.*

- *Carrie Nation was not content with choosing a **teetotaling** life for herself; instead, she won her place in history with her habit of wielding her hatchet in public taverns.*

2. Disenfranchise (dis-en-FRAN-chize)

To be disenfranchised is, primarily, to lose the right to vote. The root word is *frank,* meaning "free."

- *Those convicted of felonies suffer the additional penalty of being **disenfranchised**.*

- *The threat of **disenfranchisement** means nothing to those who never exercise their hard-won right to vote.*

3. Expurgate (EX-purr-gate)

Purging turns literary with this verb. It means to "remove erroneous, obscene, or otherwise objectionable material from a book or other piece of writing before publication." More often than not, we hear the word **unexpurgated** to describe works that have not been tampered with by overzealous editors.

- *In the early twentieth century, one had to go to Paris to obtain **unexpurgated** copies of James Joyce's novel* Ulysses.

- *As late as the 1970s, many American schools only taught **expurgated** copies of* The Catcher in the Rye *because parents and school administrators objected to J. D. Salinger's use of foul language.*

4. Impunity (im-PYOON-it-ee)

This noun means "exemption from punishment or harm." There is no such word as *punity;* we use *punishment.*

- *In his ill-received poem "Sordello," the nineteenth-century British poet Robert Browning wrote, "Any nose may ravage with **impunity** a rose."*

- *"In celebration of our last day of school, you may eat cupcakes and doughnuts in the classroom with **impunity**," announced Mrs. Marm. "Just make sure you clean up after yourselves or you'll get in trouble with the principal for making a mess."*

5. Misnomer (mis-NO-mer)

This noun refers to an inappropriate or inaccurate name for a person or thing.

- *To say I made eye contact with him would be a **misnomer**, for I found myself entranced by his bushy eyebrows and could not quit staring at them.*

- *When I asked Mr. Monaghan to name his best student, he replied, "It's Lucinda Poor—what a **misnomer**! She's anything but 'poor.'"*

As late as the 1970s, many American schools only taught **expurgated** *copies of* The Catcher in the Rye *because parents and school administrators objected to J. D. Salinger's use of foul language.*

6. Nondescript (non-dih-SCRIPT)

If something is nondescript, it lacks distinctive qualities; it's bland.

- *A criminal is less likely to be apprehended if his appearance is **nondescript**: average height, average weight, average coloring, and an absence of distinctive marks.*

- *Moby-Dick, Melville's famous fictional whale, was the opposite of **nondescript**: his whiteness was noticed by every whaler in his vicinity.*

7. Tacit (TASS-it)

If you have a tacit understanding with someone, no words are needed. You've silently understood each other.

- *The hostess wasted no time in questioning the arriving guests about their needs but **tacitly** set about making them feel welcome and comfortable.*

- *Old friends have a **tacit** understanding of each other's need to talk or to be silent.*

8. Nugatory (NOO-gat-or-ee)

This adjective originally comes from the Latin word for "jokes" or "trifles," but it has come to mean "of little or no importance" or "trifling." When you make something nugatory, you render it "futile" or "invalid." It has nothing to do with the word *nugget*.

- *"Now that you're in tennis camp, you will spend all of your time strengthening your serve and improving your speed," said Lars, the tennis pro. "All* *other activities—including eating, drinking, and sleeping—are **nugatory**."*

- *The new administration's lax environmental policies will render **nugatory** all of the previous laws regarding carbon dioxide emissions.*

9. Sinecure (SYNE-ek-yur or SIN-ek-yur)

This noun means "a job or similar position that provides a salary but little work"—a great deal if you can get it.

- *Kareem's position as the ambassador of goodwill was little more than a **sinecure**; he was paid well and given a beautiful apartment in town, but he rarely had to offer his goodwill to either visitors or natives.*

- *Damian was officially hired to be a landscape gardener at Shea Stadium, but the position turned out to be a **sinecure**: he was able to watch all of the Mets games for free but did very little actual gardening.*

10. Impasse (IM-pass)

If you're at an impasse, you can go no further: you're at a literal or figurative dead end.

- *The jury apologetically reported to the judge that their deliberations were at an **impasse**; they just couldn't reach a consensus.*

- *Gil and Maria sadly agreed that their relationship had reached an **impasse**: their individual hopes for the future were just too different.*

12 powerful words

One of Rudyard Kipling's stories contains the line "Words are, of course, the most powerful drug used by mankind," so let's have some powerful words to use in talking or writing about power, whether it comes—to give only a few possibilities—as a marching army, as a firm hand in a velvet glove, or as a strong political message.

1. Nemesis (NEM-uh-sis)

In Greek mythology, the goddess of vengeance and retribution was Nemesis. The noun means "an opponent that cannot be beaten or overcome" or "a source of harm or ruin."

- *Throughout the comic book series, Superman was plagued by his **nemesis**, Lex Luthor.*

- *"Chocolate is my **nemesis**," declared Johanna. "Even when I am on a diet, I can't resist it, so I never lose any weight."*

2. Martinet (mar-tin-ET)

This noun refers to a person who demands strict adherence to all regulations, however trivial. Its use was originally limited to the field of military endeavor, but today martinets can be found almost anywhere.

- *In the film* Dead Poets' Society *the teacher, played by Robin Williams, encourages his young charges to rebel against* **martinets** *they encounter in their classrooms.*

- *As an office supervisor, Ms. Jennings prides herself on what she calls "running a tight ship"; those unfortunate enough to work for her see her as a cruel* **martinet.**

3. Hegemony (huh-JEM-uh-nee)

Many wars are fought over power—over what state will have hegemony over another. This noun, which became very trendy in the late twentieth century, means just that: "predominant influence of one nation over another." The origin is the Greek word for "leader."

- *The movie* Dr. Strangelove *satirically displays the leaders of the United States and Russia having to choose between* **hegemony** *and survival.*

- *Athenian* **hegemony** *first emerged in the aftermath of the wars with Persia.*

4. Jeremiad (jer-uh-MY-ad)

This noun refers to a speech or written work that mournfully laments the wrongdoings of mankind and predicts a kind of wholesale doom to descend on all people. The bitter tone is associated with the writings of the Hebrew prophet Jeremiah (seventh and sixth centuries BCE), who lamented man's evil ways. Today it may be transferred to a lighter variety of doleful complaints.

- *The sociology class seemed to be going pretty well until the last week of the term, when Prof. Ausmus inexplicably broke into a kind of **jeremiad** about "your generation," calling us self-centered and self-serving.*

- *Some African American writers in the 1960s thought James Baldwin's **jeremiad** of despair left little room for the possibilities of hope and change in racial relations.*

5. Virago (veer-AH-go)

This noun refers to a woman seen as either bossy and domineering or strong and courageous; context or viewpoint determines which. It derives from the Latin word for "man."

- *Casper Milquetoast scribbled in his diary, "I am surrounded by vicious **viragos**. If only I had the courage to stand up to them!"*

- *The **Virago** Press specializes in the printing of literature by women.*

*When Thomas Carlyle wrote of the French Revolution, he referred to Marie Antoinette as "the fair young queen, the **cynosure** of all eyes."*

6. Dogmatic (dog-MAT-ik)

Though it comes from the Greek word that means "opinion," this word has a more negative connotation. Someone who is dogmatic stubbornly asserts an opinion that is unproved or not provable. Those beliefs are called **dogma**, and the person asserting them is a **dogmatist**.

- *Spouting religious **dogma**, the zealot called the college students "immoral sinners" and told them they would "never enter the Kingdom of Heaven."*

- *A **dogmatic** conservative, the president refused to raise taxes even though key social service programs were woefully underfunded.*

7. Rebarbative (re-BARB-ih-tiv)

This adjective describes something repelling, something that irritates, such as, say, rubbing your cheek against the prickly stubble of a beard. Yes, the root word is the Latin for "beard" (as in *barber*).

- *In his later years, Nasby became increasingly **rebarbative**, often answering a friendly query such as, "How are you today?" with a sarcastic rebuff like, "Who wants to know?"*

- *While Edmund has his **rebarbative** moments, he can also be welcoming and friendly; the trick is to catch him in a good mood.*

8. Redoubtable (re-DOUT-uh-bul)

Don't try to guess the meaning of this adjective, for the person it describes arouses, depending on the context, either fear or respect. That kind of person isn't usually given to self-doubt!

- *In the seventeenth century the English Parliament summoned the* **redoubtable** *Oliver Cromwell to lead their forces against the Royalist Army.*

- *Because Prof. Castillo was intolerant of error and demanded exacting precision of her students, they learned a lot, even though they found her personally* **redoubtable,** *not the type of teacher with whom they might have an informal chat.*

9. Stentorian (sten-TOR-ee-un)

This is a fancy adjective meaning "extremely loud speech." It is an eponym (a word derived from the name of a person), coming from Stentor, a Greek herald in Homer's *Iliad* whose voice was said to be as loud as the voices of fifty men combined.

- *Why do those who use their cell phones in public places tend to be so* **stentorian***?*

- *In earlier eras the ability to be* **stentorian** *was prized, but in this day of microphones and public address systems it is not required.*

10. Cynosure (SY-no-sure)

A cynosure is something or someone that everyone looks at; an earlier use was limited to something, such as the North Star, that people use to guide and direct them (so, obviously, they have to look at it). (All you lovers of word history, get yourself to a dictionary to understand why *cynosure* literally means "dog's tail"!)

- *Even students who considered themselves "celebrity-proof" felt the* **cynosural** *power of the star of* Saturday Night Live *as he made his way through the lobby and hallways of the school, heading for the auditorium where he would speak on techniques of satire.*

- *When Thomas Carlyle wrote of the French Revolution, he referred to Marie Antoinette as "the fair young queen, the* **cynosure** *of all eyes."*

13 repeating words

Repetition can be delightful or boring, depending on who is doing the repeating and what it is they keep doing or saying. These ten words offer a variety of possibilities.

1. **Recidivist** (ree-SID-iv-ist)

From the Latin word for "to fall back," this noun means "someone who returns to a previous pattern of behavior, especially criminal behavior." The adjective form is **recidivistic**.

- *The Department of Motor Vehicles punishes* **recidivists** *more severely than first-time offenders. Drivers who are caught for moving violations must pay more for each succeeding ticket.*

- *The American Cancer Society suggests different measures for* **recidivistic** *smokers, ranging from hypnosis to nicotine patches.*

2. **Doppelganger** (DOP-el-gang-er)

From the German for "double-goer," this noun means "a ghostly double of a living person," usually one that stalks or haunts its real-life counterpart.

- *Joseph Conrad's novella* The Secret Sharer *is about a sea captain who is haunted by a* **doppelganger**, *a naked swimmer named Leggatt, who mysteriously comes aboard his ship and shares all of the intimate details of his life.*

- *Clothilde was increasingly bothered by Holly, who became her* **doppelganger**, *dressing like her, wearing her hair in the same style, and even taking a job in the same advertising agency.*

3. Tautology (taw-TOL-oh-jee)

Like *redundancy* (see #4), this noun means "a needless repetition of the same words or phrases." It can also be used to describe an empty statement composed of simple statements that make it *logically* true, whether the simple statements are *factually* true or not.

- *"The general consensus of opinion" and "7 a.m. in the morning" are both* **tautologies;** *one only needs to say "the consensus" and "7 a.m."*

- *"I am either in love with you or I'm crazy about you," Harry said, offering a meaningless* **tautology** *rather than an expression of his deepest feelings.*

4. Redundant (re-DUN-dunt)

This adjective describes something that exceeds what's necessary; it's a synonym for *superfluous*. The root word is the Latin word *unda,* meaning "a wave," so something redundant is like that second wave that knocks you over as you're getting up from the first.

- *Wearing a belt and suspenders is not only unfashionable, it's highly **redundant**.*

- *It annoys John Simon, that precise user of words, when people use the **redundant** phrase "refer back to." "Refer" in itself, he might say impatiently, means "carry back."*

5. Simulacrum (sim-ul-AK-rum)

This fancy noun means "image" or "representation" in both English and Latin; it uses its Latin plural **simulacra**. The verb *simulate*—"to imitate"—is in the same family.

- *The artist made paintings of a number of photographs and titled the series* Double **Simulacra** *#1–#7.*

- *Louis Auchincloss describes Woodrow Wilson, when he returned to office after his stroke, as being but a **simulacrum** of his former self.*

*"And then she spoke to him with her lips," wrote the poet Virgil, quite deliberately choosing the **pleonasm**.*

6. Palimpsest (PAL-imp-sest)

This fascinating and complex word refers to either a literal manuscript, possibly on hide or parchment, that has been written on, scraped, and written on again, or an object or place that similarly reflects layers of its history.

- *We're accustomed to thinking of Rome as a **palimpsest** of classical, medieval, Renaissance, and modern life, but Professor Limerick's lecture on Tucson, Arizona, has helped me see that southwestern city with its layering of Indian, Hispanic, and Anglo life in a similar light.*

- *Dr. Ulanov was ecstatic when the vellum manuscript he purchased inexpensively in an Athens marketplace turned out to be a **palimpsest** with some recoverable diagrams by Archimedes on a lower layer.*

7. Pleonasm (PLEE-o-nazm)

This noun is an elegant linguistic term for a verbal redundancy; sometimes it occurs through ignorance, but it can be deliberately used for poetic effect.

- *"Widow woman" is a good example of a colloquial **pleonasm**: all widows are female.*

- *"And then she spoke to him with her lips," wrote the poet Virgil, quite deliberately choosing the **pleonasm**.*

8. Verisimilitude (ver-a-sim-IL-a-tude)

This noun names a condition of likeness to truth, similarity to reality.

- *Jonathan Swift, whose brilliant essay "A Modest Proposal" imitates the style of economic proposals of the era, opens with mind-numbing statistics to create an air of **verisimilitude**.*

- *The women's knee-length dresses with long strings of pearls and the men's straw boater hats created a* sense of **verisimilitude** *at the Gatsby party hosted by Carole's English class.*

9. Reiterate (re-IT-er-ate)

This verb means, simply, "to repeat." The noun form is **reiteration**.

- *"Let me **reiterate**," intoned the professor. "To pass this course, you must turn in all papers on time."*

- *"It's true that everything meaningful has already been said," noted Tom philosophically, "but **reiteration** is necessary because you may have a new way to put it, and, besides, not everyone was listening the first time around."*

10. Recrudescent (ree-kru-DESS-ent)

This adjective means "to revivify" or "to come back to life after a period of quiet inactivity." The verb form is **recrudesce**.

- *After a long summer of lazy beach days and afternoon naps, Walter Jimcrack is **recrudescent** and ready to reassume his position as the vigilant security guard at P.S. 117 in the South Bronx.*

- *Like a phoenix emerging from the ashes, Arnold **recrudesced**, returning to his job as a construction worker after suffering what his doctors thought might be a fatal brain tumor.*

14 riddling words

In the days of early English, what we call a *sieve* was called a *riddil*, and we still see that meaning in this usage: "His argument was riddled with inconsistencies." But the words below are more akin to the "puzzle" meaning of *riddle*— words that express something not immediately clear.

1. Enigma (en-IG-ma)

An enigma is a puzzling, inexplicable, or ambiguous situation. You can use it to describe a person (the adjective form is **enigmatic**) or a thing.

- *In a 1939 radio broadcast, British statesman Winston Churchill said: "I cannot forecast to you the action of Russia. It is a riddle wrapped in a mystery inside an **enigma**."*

- *Professor Arfer's grading policies were a complete **enigma** to his students; he seemed to weigh class participation, attendance, and exam grades in different combinations each semester.*

2. Ambiguous (am-BIG-yoo-us)

You probably know the prefix *ambi-* ("either, both"), as in *ambidextrous*, meaning (roughly) that both hands are "right" hands. *Ambiguous* suggests that the meaning of something is uncertain, open to more than one interpretation. The noun form is **ambiguity**.

- *The ending of the novel both fascinates and perplexes because the wording is so **ambiguous**: the reader has to decide if Gerald plunges off the cliff or retreats to the car.*

- *The ability to tolerate **ambiguity** may be a characteristic of maturity: the poet John Keats called this capacity "negative capability."*

3. Ambivalent (am-BIV-a-lent)

The prefix *ambi-* means "both," and *valence* is "attraction," so ambivalent feelings involve near-equal attraction to two or more choices, or mixed attraction and repulsion to one thing. Situations and statements may be ambiguous, but human emotions are ambivalent.

- *Monica is feeling totally **ambivalent** about buying a house: she likes the idea of permanence but fears the responsibility of a mortgage.*

- *"You'll probably always have some **ambivalence** about important decisions," Thea wisely counseled.*

4. Byzantine (BIZ-uhn-teen)

Sometimes capitalized, this adjective is in increasingly common use to describe something excessively complicated, especially when the complexities come about through intrigue or scheming. The origin, of course, lies in the word *Byzantine* as referring to the eastern part of the later Roman Empire. Was the Byzantine Empire byzantine?

- *Although the company has very few written rules, the informal structure is **byzantine**, leaving new employees bewildered until they figure out whom to see about what.*

- *Sociologists are increasingly interested in the rather **byzantine** social codes of preadolescent girls: if Millie insults Mollie, will Maggie snub Millie?*

5. Paradox (PAIR-uh-dox)

A paradox is a seemingly contradictory statement, one that probably reveals a truth. The adjective form is **paradoxical**.

- *However **paradoxical** it may seem, love and hate can coexist.*

- *It is a **paradox** that most of the greatest novelists have never formally studied creative writing.*

*The ability to tolerate **ambiguity** may be a characteristic of maturity: the poet John Keats called this capacity "negative capability."*

6. Labyrinthine (lab-er-IN-thin or lab-er-IN-theen)

If you remember the maze that confined the minotaur in Greek mythology, then you'll understand this adjective. It describes something that has the qualities of a **labyrinth** or maze—an intricate structure of interconnected passages. Like something that is convoluted, something that is labyrinthine can be very confusing. It describes situations or places, not people.

- *The inside of the school was so **labyrinthine** that Megan could not find her way to her history class and wandered the halls for hours.*

- *Christos's excuse was so **labyrinthine** that no one was convinced that he was innocent.*

7. Conundrum (cuh-NUN-drum)

A conundrum is a challenging puzzle, a dilemma, a riddle. Even the origin of the word is unknown.

- *Bert accidentally goofed up his electronic calendar and realized he has two social engagements at the same hour on Friday night; he's now dealing with the **conundrum** of which to cancel.*

- *"I'll never understand Al," sighed Jan. "He'll always be a complete **conundrum** to me."*

8. Oneiric (o-NYE-rik)

Few things are more puzzling than dreams. This word is the scholarly adjective for matters that relate to or suggest dreams or visions.

- *While the painting has realistic elements, overall it possesses an **oneiric** quality; it gives the viewer the feeling of something partially or imperfectly remembered.*

- *The ruler valued Tasmario for his reputed **oneiric** interpretations: Tasmario, however, knew that flattery helped make his analyses believable.*

9. Oxymoron (ox-e-MOR-on)

An oxymoron is a brief paradox, a word or phrase that seems to contradict itself but does not. The word itself literally means "sharp dullness." The adjective form is **oxymoronic**.

- *I call myself a cheerful pessimist, however **oxymoronic** that may sound.*

- *As second-year students are often reminded, the word "sophomore" is an **oxymoron**: it literally means "wise fool."*

10. Latent (LATE-unt)

If it's latent, it's present, but not evident, so you may or may not know it's there.

- *The doctor told Tony he had a **latent** infection; strengthening his immune system might eliminate any need for medication.*

- *Sarah's triumphant stage debut in the spring play should be credited to the director, the first person to recognize and encourage her **latent** talent.*

15 hodgepodge

Like its two random predecessors, this chapter offers ten fine words that are not related by a theme.

1. Narcissist (NAR-sis-ist)

A negative word for those people who are more than a little too into themselves. Narcissists, as they are in love with themselves, lack empathy with others. The word comes from Greek mythology; Narcissus fell in love with his reflection in a pool, and in punishment he was turned into a flower—a very pretty flower. The noun form is **narcissism**.

- *Some sociologists believe we are developing a culture of **narcissism**, what with the rise of the "self-esteem" movement and the growing popularity of blogs that chronicle the lives of average individuals in excruciating detail.*

- *"If you feel you're falling in love with a **narcissist**," counseled Dr. Dougherty, "run the other way, head for the hills. It's a prescription for disaster."*

2. Iconoclastic (i-kon-oh-KLASS-tik)

This word describes a person (an **iconoclast**) who seeks to overthrow popular ideas or institutions, which takes a certain amount of temerity. It comes from the Medieval Greek meaning "smasher of religious images." The noun form is **iconoclasm**.

- *Ever the **iconoclast**, Stephen was the only student in class who believed that cell phones were a foolish invention and a waste of money.*

- *Nietzsche revealed his **iconoclasm** when he announced to his nineteenth-century readers that God is dead.*

3. Supercilious (soo-per-SIL-ee-us)

This delightful adjective means "haughty." Its etymology will help you remember it: it roughly means "with a raised eyebrow," so you can picture the arch expression on the face of someone with a supercilious attitude.

- *When the ill-mannered diner shouted at the headwaiter in the elegant restaurant, "Whadda I have to do to get some water in this joint?" the latter **superciliously** replied, "You might, sir, try setting yourself on fire."*

- *An occasional **supercilious** remark can delight by its wit, but few people enjoy the company of the haughty for long.*

4. Visceral (VISS-er-al)

Descriptive of an emotional reaction that is deep, nearly instinctive, as if experienced in the intestines of the body, the *viscera*. In short, a (literally) "gut response."

- *When an insensitive acquaintance parodied her favorite poem, Suellyn felt a **visceral** disgust.*

- *Should we act on our **visceral** responses or should we regard intellectual analysis as more important?*

5. Serendipity (serr-in-DIP-uh-tee)

How happy we are that there's a word for the fortunate event of finding something you like even though you weren't actively looking for it! If you agree, send up a moment of thanks to eighteenth-century English writer Horace Walpole, who minted the term from an old Persian fairy tale about princes from Serendip, a place in Sri Lanka.

- *Olivia and Caitlin named their store **Serendipity** because they hoped the whimsical items in the shop would appeal to affluent customers who were looking for something to want.*

- *"I searched for the pickle fork missing from my grandmother's silver pattern for years before I gave up," mused Annalee, "then one day, at an antiques fair, there it was—what **serendipity**!"*

*Nietzsche revealed his **iconoclasm** when he announced to his nineteenth-century readers that God is dead.*

6. Gemütlich (geh-MOOT-lick)

As you've likely guessed, this adjective comes into English from German. It fills a gap in the English word hoard by describing, in one word, an atmosphere or feeling of warm, cozy, comfortable happiness. The noun form, **gemütlichkeit**, also keeps its Germanic form.

- *Although some of his fellow passengers on the cruise grated on his nerves, Seymour mostly enjoyed the* **gemütlich** *atmosphere of the small groups that gathered for brandy after dinner.*

- *When asked why she was skipping the company picnic, Margaret snorted, "Compulsory* **gemütlichkeit**? *Not my cup of tea!"*

7. Iridescent (ear-ih-DESS-unt)

This adjective describes the appearance of a shining spectrum of colors. Its meaning and spelling (only one *r*) are easy to remember when you know the word comes from Iris, the classical goddess of the rainbow. The noun form is **iridescence**.

- *Young John marveled at the* **iridescent** *display of colors in the feathers of so common a bird as the pigeon.*

- *Photographers find beauty in unexpected places, such as the* **iridescence** *of an oil slick.*

8. Sybarite (SIB-uh-rite)

This noun, which can be used admiringly or critically, fits an individual whose life is given over to pleasure and luxury. It has its origin in an ancient Greek city, Sybaris, notorious for its luxurious excess. The adjective form is **sybaritic**.

- *"Those who criticize our **sybaritic** existence are merely envious," said Lady Gotalot, as she sent her footman out for caviar and peacocks' tongues.*

- *Being a counselor in many Girl Scout camps is great fun, but not for **sybarites**; you may be asked to shower in cold water and to sleep on an army cot.*

9. Patina (PAT-uh-nuh or puh-TEE-nuh)

Literally, this noun refers to a greenish overlay that can form on copper or bronze. It's also used figuratively to mean any kind of surface covering.

- *Harville, the antiques dealer, was horrified when a customer asked if the **patina** on the statue of Mercury could be removed before it was delivered to her home. "Madame," he said, "it attests to the age of the work and thus makes it more valuable."*

- *Underneath Grover's **patina** of shyness is a fascinating and kind personality.*

10. Gnomic (NOME-ik)

This has nothing to do with those little creatures in some people's gardens! This adjective describes a brief encapsulation of a truth, a pithy aphorism. Often gnomic statements express wisdom, but they can be annoyingly affected.

- *The inscription on the Greek temple at Delphi—"Know thyself"—is a good example of a **gnomic** saying.*

- *Whenever family members asked Sandy about his plans for the week, he answered with a maddeningly **gnomic** "You'll see."*

Quiz #3

CATEGORY A

Match each definition on the right with the appropriate word in the column on the left.

_____ stentorian A. bitter complaint or prophecy

_____ sinecure B. manuscript written on more than once

_____ jeremiad C. extremely loud

_____ palimpsest D. twisting, winding

_____ labyrinthine E. a plum job, with little work

CATEGORY B

Select a word from the list below that best fits each of the sentences on the next page. (One sentence calls for two words.) Some words won't be used at all.

impunity **tautology**

doppelganger **oxymoron**

recidivist **cynosure**

redundant **redoubtable**

paradox

1. His behavior is something of a _____; he says he's for gun control, but owns several weapons himself.

2. Because a brief is often not brief at all (but just the opposite), the lawyers may have invented the only one-word _____ in our language.

3. He thought he could commit more crimes with _____, but soon found himself back in jail, a _____.

4. When McSweeney tried to convince the judge that the criminal had been someone who looked a lot like him, his _____, the judge's response was somewhat supercilious.

5. If you say "refer back," people who know that *re-* means "back" will say you're being _____.

CATEGORY C

1. Some employees think he's such a martinet at work because his wife is such a virago at home. What kind of behavior would you expect from the husband? The wife?

2. Almost all the comments he makes on my drafts are completely nugatory. How does the writer feel about the comments?

3. His behavior is marked by the patina of conformity; underneath he's an iconoclast. Explain.

4. The sports reporter asked the tennis star, "Any visceral feelings about your upcoming match with your nemesis Ace Lane?" What might the athlete's reply be?

5. Thomas Bowdler contributed a new word to our language when he published an expurgated version of Shakespeare's works. What did Bowdler do to the works?

16
scholarly words

It's unlikely that you'll be using any of these words over a cup of coffee with your friends. But you'll feel good that you know their meanings when you see them on the page of a learned book or hear them in a lecture.

1. Exegesis (ex-uh-JEE-sus)

This noun is a learned way to refer to a critical analysis, especially of a literary or Biblical test. The plural is **exegeses**.

- *The professor asked each member of the class to give an **exegesis** of the account of creation in the book of Genesis.*

- *Marta's **exegesis** of the opening ten lines of Shakespeare's* Hamlet *brought out aspects of the character of Francisco that would never have entered my mind.*

2. Polysemous (pol-lee-SEE-mus)

This adjective describes something, usually a text, that has many interpretations. The two root words are the familiar prefix *poly-*, meaning "many," and the Greek root for the word *sign*, which you'll see in the related words **semantics** (the study of meaning, particularly in language) and **semiotics** (the theory and study of signs and symbols, particularly within language).

- *Bulgakov's novel* The Master and Margarita *can be termed **polysemous** because of the linking of aspects of its four different and complex plots.*

- *Former President Bill Clinton's **semantic** concern with the meaning of the word "is" is part of an often-quoted line.*

3. Dionysian (dye-a-NEE-see-un)

Along with its partner word below, this adjective alludes to a split described by the nineteenth-century philosopher Friedrich Nietzsche between the creative or intuitive force, as symbolized by the Greek god Dionysus, and the power of rationality, as symbolized by the Greek god Apollo.

- *The comic satyr play that was performed after three tragedies in ancient Athenian festivals may represent a reminder of the power of the **dionysian** to break the spell of the rational.*

- *When hard-working college students let off a little steam in Saturday night off-campus parties, are they simply continuing the long **dionysian** tradition?*

4. Apollonian (ap-uh-LOAN-ee-un)

See the complementary partner for this word above. Apollo, the namesake of the word, was the god associated with the power of critical reasoning. (Both words are often capitalized.)

- *Charlotte Brontë's heroine Jane Eyre is more attracted to the stormy Mr. Rochester than to the **apollonian** St. John Rivers, who offers her plenty of good reasons why he and she should marry.*

- *"It's not 'either/or,'" Prof. Levine wisely counseled her students. Society needs both the energy of the **dionysian** and the restraint of the **apollonian**."*

5. Iconography (eye-kun-OG-raf-ee)

This noun literally means "the writing of images" and is used, particularly within the history of art, to refer to the study and interpretation of visual images and patterns.

- *Those who know nothing about Christianity will have trouble interpreting the **iconography** of medieval paintings, such as the fact that a lion frequently symbolizes the apostle Mark.*

- *When Mary Helen first arrived on the Gothic campus of her university, her attention was immediately captured by carvings on the buildings; her study of the **iconography** helped deepen her appreciation of the history of the institution.*

6. Historiography (hiss-tor-ee-OG-raf-ee)

There's history and then there's historiography. The latter word is a scholarly term for an organized look at the way history comes to be written.

- *Josephine Tey's detective with a broken leg becomes an amateur **historiographer** when he starts to compare and interpret all the sources for the demonization of the fifteenth-century ruler Richard III.*

- *"The record of a conflict is written by the winner" is an often-quoted maxim of those interested in **historiography**.*

*Charlotte Brontë's heroine Jane Eyre is more attracted to the stormy Mr. Rochester than to the **apollonian** St. John Rivers, who offers her plenty of good reasons why he and she should marry.*

7. Epistemology (e-pis-ta-MOL-uh-jee)

This is a very learned word for the branch of philosophy dealing with the nature of knowledge.

- *While **epistemology** seems a rarefied concept, the questions of how we learn and how we know what we know confront classroom teachers everyday.*

- *The French philosopher Descartes, most famous for his statement "I think; therefore I am," is a good exemplar of a rational **epistemologist**.*

8. Hermeneutics (her-muh-NEW-tics)

This example of what Shakespeare might term an "inkhorn word" is frequently heard in academic settings. It refers to the theory and method of interpretation, particularly of texts. The adjective form **hermeneutic** is a scholarly synonym for *interpretive* or *explanatory*.

- *The graduate students in the comparative literature class were asked to give **hermeneutic** rationales for their explications of the texts.*

- *Considering the stated intention of an author was virtually forbidden in Prof. Corso's class: he encouraged a **hermeneutics** based only on the words in the poem.*

9. Dialectics (dye-uh-LEK-tiks)

Not related to the word *dialect* (regional variations in vocabulary and pronunciation), this scholarly term refers to the weighing of seemingly contradictory facts or ideas with an attempt to resolve their opposition.

- ***Dialectics** is important in interpreting Shakespeare's* Hamlet: *virtually all the characters contain something of the commandingly powerful and something of the touchingly vulnerable.*

- *The German philosopher Hegel used **dialectics** in his formation of the idea of weighing a thesis and its antithesis together in expectation of arriving at a synthesis.*

10. Postmodern (post-MOD-ern)

This adjective, now widely used in discussions of literature, art, and architecture, defies simple explanation. Briefly, it describes something that reacts against "modernism" either by reintroducing classical elements or by carrying modernist practices to an extreme. The noun form is **postmodernism**.

- *Would Robert Rauschenberg's ground-breaking sculpture involving a stuffed goat and a tire be a good example of **postmodernism**?*

- *Using those classical Greek columns for the front of his three-car garage is just one example of Ridley's **postmodern** sense of humor.*

shape-shifting words

Teiresias, in ancient Greek myth, was sometimes male, sometimes female. Lycanthropes can change between human and wolf (we know them better as werewolves). Yes, true shape-shifters belong to the realm of folktales and literature, but there are plenty of interesting words that describe less dramatic changes in form.

1. **Metamorphosis** (met-a-MORF-oh-sis)

This noun means "a complete transformation in appearance, character, or function." The plural is **metamorphoses**. It often suggests a change that occurs by magic or sorcery, as in the mythological stories recounted in Ovid's *Metamorphoses*.

- *According to Ovid, the gods **metamorphosed** the handsome Narcissus into a flower after he stood by a pool for a long time, admiring his reflection.*

- *Dina's **metamorphosis** into a beautiful young woman occurred after a particularly awkward and painful adolescence.*

2. Anthropomorphic (an-thro-po-MORF-ik)

Using the same root word *morph* or "shape" as metamorphosis, this adjective refers to something that is not human but seems to have taken on the form of a human. (*Anthropo-* is the same root that gives us *anthropology*, the study of mankind.)

- *"Your concept of God is **anthropomorphic**," said Laetitia. "Where you see an elderly man with a beard up in the heavens, I prefer to think of the Divine as formless, totally a spirit."*

- *The pigs in George Orwell's* Animal Farm *are almost completely **anthropomorphic**: while they retain a piglike appearance, they think, talk, and scheme like not very admirable humans.*

Bonus word: the opposite of anthropomorphic is **theriomorphic**—shaped like an animal.

- *Art Spiegelman's* Maus *is **theriomorphic** in that Jewish prisoners in World War II are depicted as mice while their Nazi captors are large cats.*

3. Attenuate (ah-TEN-you-ate)

This verb means "to reduce in force, value, size, or degree." It comes from the Latin for "to make thin." A verb with a similar meaning is *truncate*, but it is used only to mean "to shorten."

- *Niko's robust health was **attenuated** by poor eating habits, lack of exercise, and his high-stress job as an emergency medical technician.*

- *Sloane's anger at her boyfriend **attenuated** with every bouquet and note of apology he sent.*

4. Transmogrify (trans-MOG-ri-fie)

This verb describes a radical change of shape (possibly humorous or bizarre), either literal or figurative. Its origins are uncertain but may be related to the word *migrate*.

- *Many an English major has first encountered this word in John Crowe Ransom's poem "Janet Waking," in which a **transmogrifying** bee changes life into death.*

- *"Where did my sweet children go?" queried Mrs. Tate as her twins reached adolescence. "Sybil has gone from pink to punk while Bryan has **transmogrified** himself into some junior reincarnation of Ozzy Osbourne."*

5. Abrogate (AB-ro-gate)

Something that is abrogated is abolished or done away with. Don't confuse this word with the similar-sounding **abridge**, which has the less drastic meaning of "shorten."

- *"Under the current administration," said the head of the city council, "our civic rights have been completely **abrogated**."*

- *"Did you read the Harry Potter series?" sneered Zander annoyingly, "or are you waiting for an **abridged**, easy-reading version to come out?*

*The pigs in George Orwell's
Animal Farm are almost completely
anthropomorphic: while they retain
a piglike appearance, they think,
talk, and scheme like not very
admirable humans.*

6. Truncate (TRUN-kate)

If you truncate something, you shorten it, often in an abrupt manner. (Memory hook: you cut off the head and legs and leave only the *trunk*.)

- *Plans for a twelve-part, federally funded television series on the origin of words were severely **truncated** after the influential Senator Buncombe argued that one program could cover all anyone needed to know about words.*

- *Lucy and Willy's plans to join their friends for an all-night round of clubbing were **truncated** when they made the mistake of answering their dad's call on their cell phone.*

7. Dilate (DIE-late)

The process of **dilation** makes something wider or larger. You may know the literal sense of the word from the eye-doctor's office, but it can also be used in a figurative sense, particularly in reference to talking or writing a lot.

- *While the pupils of his eyes were still **dilated,** Robin needed dark glasses to drive in the bright sunlight.*

- Saxo Grammaticus, *an early source of the* Hamlet *story,* **dilates** *on qualities of Hamlet's personality that are not emphasized in Shakespeare's play.*

8. Curtail (ker-TAIL)

To curtail something is to cut it short, to reduce it in size. A good one-word near-synonym is the verb **dock.** It's often used in reference to salary.

- *"Let's **curtail** this discussion," suggested Jerome, "and resume when we've all regained our senses of humor."*

- *Ms. McMuffin's wages will be **docked** until she has repaid the company for the 413 boxes of paper clips she has stolen over the years.*

9. Microcosm (MIKE-ro-kozm)

Not exactly a shape-shifter, this noun is very useful for something that is a small representation of a larger unit: Its Greek roots literally mean "small world." Its useful twin is **macrocosm**, which means the counterpart, a "big world" analogous with some smaller unit.

- *Would you agree that the economic well-being of the auto industry is a **microcosm** of the health of the national economy?*

- *During the heyday of the monarchy, the country was sometimes viewed as a **macrocosm** of the person of the king.*

10. Procrustean (pro-KRUST-ee-un)

Coming from the name of the Greek mythological character Procrustes, this adjective describes something that uses ruthless means to enforce strict conformity. The literal Procrustes wanted everyone to fit his bed: those that were too short were cruelly stretched; those that were too tall were docked.

- *Mme. Une-Taille is a fine teacher of the French language, but she imposes **procrustean** control over interpretations of poems: only those that agree with hers are acceptable.*

- *Employees were happy when their company dropped its **procrustean** nine-to-five schedule of working hours and adopted a program of "flex-time" that was meant to help those with child care responsibilities outside work.*

18 short words

When we think of adding new words to our vocabulary, we're usually envisioning long words, polysyllabic words, those that have jokingly been termed *sesquipedalian* (a foot and a half long). But some useful one-syllable words aren't as well-known as they should be.

1. Wraith (rayth)

This noun is usually used as a synonym for *ghost*. In a more specialized way it can be an apparition of one who is soon to die. Occasionally, it's used by extension to mean any human form of thin and wispy appearance (such as the comic book character whose skin can turn translucent). The word history is obscure, but many guess that it's Scottish.

- *An old legend of the region claimed that **wraiths** of those to die within the year appeared in the churchyard at midnight of a certain day.*

- *Jerome's recent illness has caused him to lose so much weight that his appearance is **wraith-like**.*

2. Fop (rhymes with *stop*)

It's a noun, always critical and always reserved for males. (Don't worry about discrimination, guys; there are even more negative words reserved for females.) It's used for a man who, in a mainstream opinion, is too concerned with his looks and his clothes.

- *While Frank has great taste in clothes and a closet full of cool clothing, no one would ever call him a **fop**.*

- *In eighteenth-century England, many men with money wore patterned silk vests, velvet jackets, and shirts with lace cuffs. Anyone dressing like that today would be laughed at and deemed a **fop**.*

3. Pan (rhymes with *man*)

We're looking here at the verb *pan*, meaning "to criticize a performance severely, to find totally inadequate." Its origin invites speculation: would you like to attack a certain performance with, say, an iron skillet? (The verb *pan* is also a technical term referring to a camera shot, and is short for *panorama*.)

- *Some critics completely **panned** the new production of* King Kong, *finding it a totally unworthy successor to the illustrious original.*

- *Norm, a complete novice to the world of Shakespeare, dared not dream of rave reviews for his Falstaff; he hoped merely to avoid being **panned**.*

4. Wax (rhymes with *Max*)

We're not talking about shining your floors. Meanings of the verb *wax* are "to grow physically larger" (when you're talking about the moon), and, more generally, to take on a characteristic.

- *Alice said the moon is getting smaller this week, but she's wrong: the fact it's larger than it was three nights ago proves that it's **waxing**, not waning.*

- *Sascha earns his living as a statistician, but his passion lies elsewhere; whenever you ask him about playing the lute, he **waxes** eloquent about the history and beauty of the instrument.*

*Christopher Marlowe's play Dr. Faustus depicts the title character falling in love with a vision of Helen of Troy and marveling, "All is **dross** that is not Helena."*

5. Bilk (Billk)

This verb, meaning "to cheat or to defraud," entered the language as a slang word, but it has gained respectability. Scholars believe its origin is related to *balk* or *hesitate*. It's often used in its financial sense but can be found in other contexts.

- *As a savvy art dealer of many years' experience, Mr. Veenud was not amused at being **bilked** by Lord Fancy.*

- *Can destiny be **bilked**? Sophocles' play* Oedipus Rex *implies the answer is "no."*

6. Gaffe (rhymes with *laugh*)

A gaffe is a blunder, sometimes verbal, sometimes not.

- *The fact that the political candidate briefly confused Iran with Iraq was regarded as a major **gaffe** by his opponents.*

- *Sigmund Freud believed that linguistic **gaffes** were not slips of the tongue but promptings from the subconscious.*

7. Dross (rhymes with *floss*)

This useful noun refers to useless matter, something utterly meaningless. In terms of word history, it's akin to the monosyllable *dregs*, that useless residue at the bottom of your coffee cup.

- *Christopher Marlowe's play* Dr. Faustus *depicts the title character falling in love with a vision of Helen of Troy and marveling, "All is **dross** that is not Helena."*

- *"Don't speak to me about spreadsheets and payrolls and such **dross**," exclaimed Ian. "I'm on vacation!"*

8. Schism (SIZ-um—the traditional pronunciation—and SKIZ-um are both acceptable)

This noun refers to a split, a breach, a separation. Derived from the Greek verb meaning "to split," you can see the meaning in that medical term for a mind that is split—*schizophrenia*. You'll also see it in a religious context for situations where a split in doctrinal beliefs causes a schism (maybe best known for the Great Schism of 1054 that divided the Catholic and Orthodox churches).

- *Thanksgiving dinner is the traditional time for relatives to paper over all familial **schisms** and spend a few convivial hours together.*

- *Descartes's well-known assertion "I think; therefore I am" expresses a belief in a major **schism** between body and mind that not everyone accepts.*

9. Scourge (rhymes with *urge*)

Both a noun and a verb, this word refers to the inflicting of punishment or even devastation. (It originally referred to a whip or the act of whipping that was designed to bring about behavior more in line with the point of view of the one wielding the whip.)

- *Smallpox was once the **scourge** of the world: how fortunate we are to live in an era when it is virtually gone from the earth!*

- *Hamlet refers to himself at one point in the play as being both "**scourge** and minister," a source of both harming and healing.*

10. Fell (rhymes with *bell*)

This adjective means "cruel" or "lethal." You may know it best from the old phrase *in one fell swoop,* which many say without realizing it means "a deadly motion."

- *The stoic speaker in the well-known poem "Invictus" claims he has not winced or cried aloud "in the **fell** clutch of circumstance."*

- *By some **fell** chance the pedestrian tripped on an uneven patch of the pavement just as a huge truck roared down upon him.*

19

sinful words

We start this chapter on sinful words with three words dealing with the general concept of wrongdoing; we then follow that trio with seven words that are rough synonyms of the seven deadly sins: pride, envy, greed, anger, lust, sloth, and gluttony.

1. Hamartia (ham-art-TEE-uh)

Outside the Judeo-Christian concept of sin, this word is the classical Greek term for "serious error," sometimes oversimplified to "tragic flaw." Its literal meaning comes from archery; the idea of missing the mark on a target.

- *Aristotle writes about **hamartia** in his comments on Greek tragedy: he notes that it may be an error in judgment as well as some chronic flaw.*

- *The fourth-century CE writer Prudentius, in an allegorical poem about **hamartia,** symbolizes the corruption of language in the splitting of the tongue of the devil.*

2. Peccadillo (peck-a-DIL-oh)

A little sin, a small fault, this word comes into English from Spanish.

- *Ms. Armstrong never dreamed she could be fired for a **peccadillo** such as playing one game of solitaire on her office computer, especially a game she had lost!*

- *Fans of W. C. Fields relish his famous line, "None of your **peccadilloes**, my little chickadee."*

3. Expiate (EX-pe-ate)

This word deals with atoning for sin. The root word is the same as that for *pious,* which means "holy." It's now often used in a figurative and secular sense. The noun form is **expiation**.

- *Seeking **expiation** for his unlawful seizing of the throne, Henry IV set off on a pilgrimage to Jerusalem.*

- *After Hamford broke his wife's favorite vase, he tried to **expiate** his misdeed by buying her a new vase and filling it with her favorite yellow roses.*

4. Hubris (HUE-bris)

This classical Greek word for "an excess of pride that may lead to a downfall" can be used for both what happens within Greek tragedy and what happens in modern day life. The adjective form is **hubristic**.

- *Whenever a protagonist declares himself equal to the gods, the audience may expect that such **hubris** will be punished.*

- *Mona's claim that she'll be CEO of General Motors someday seems **hubristic,** for she has only been out of business school for three years.*

5. Invidious (in-VID-e-us)

This adjective takes on the concept of envy; it applies to remarks or actions that tend to incite envy.

- *"Why can't you be more like Paragonia?" is not a comment that any wise parent of more than one child would ever make; such **invidious** comparisons cause much harm.*

- *Agamemnon found it an **invidious** matter to have to make a distinction among the bravest and most skilled of his soldiers.*

*Aristotle writes about **hamartia** in his comments on Greek tragedy: he notes that it may be an error in judgment as well as some chronic flaw.*

6. Avaricious (av-uh-RISH-us)

This adjective speaks of an excessive desire for money; every individual may have a different definition of when "acceptable" becomes "too much."

- *Chaucer's "Pardoner's Tale" deals with three thieves whose **avarice** causes them to steal and then to die in* an attempt to cheat their comrades out of their share of the loot.

- *A cartoonish image of **avarice** is the miser who takes delight in the physical handling and counting of the money that he stores under his narrow bed.*

7. Apoplectic (ap-o-PLEC-tic)

Literally, this adjective refers to the bodily affliction of **apoplexy**, a neurological impairment like a stroke. More usefully, though, it means "full of rage," and you'll frequently hear it as a synonym for *furious*.

- *When Dewitt's girlfriend told him she wanted to break up, he grew **apoplectic,** failing to comprehend that his quick rage was the main reason she wanted to end the relationship.*

- *"I don't 'get' road rage," said Mariella. "Someone cuts you off on the interstate and you get all **apoplectic**? Why?"*

8. Libido (lih-BEE-doh)

This is the rather formal term for sexual desire. (One can't imagine lovers saying it to each other, except in jest.)

- *While Othello is very much in love with his wife, his **libido** takes second place to his need to feel no other man could take his place in her affections.*

- *The class was studying Freud's three-layered structure of the psyche: the superego, the ego, and the id, the last of these three being the site of the **libido**.*

9. Enervated (EN-er-vayt-ed)

This adjective (from the verb **enervate**) describes a sense of weakened vitality, a loss of energy, causing you to feel as if some vital nerve had been removed.

- *After the soccer team lost to their archrival, Jason, the team captain, felt **enervated**, not so much from physical exhaustion as from emotional depletion.*

- *Many Roman leaders believed that an excess of luxury had **enervated** civilizations such as Egypt and that too much contact with these nations could **enervate** Rome itself.*

10. Gourmand (goor-MOND)

As it's used most of the time, the word is a synonym for *glutton*. (Occasionally, you'll see it in the more neutral sense of "lover of fine food," but its linguistic cousin *gourmet* is the better choice for that meaning.)

- *Philip does love good food, but you'd have to label him a **gourmand**: even in expensive restaurants he orders several entrées to be sure of sampling the chef's specialties.*

- *If Dante's vision of Hell should turn out to be literally accurate, **gourmands** from all centuries may be amazed to find themselves punished more harshly than adulterers.*

20 olio

An olio (O-lee-o), from the Spanish word *olla* ("pot"), is a stew—often a mixture of different meats, fish, and vegetables. The word is also in common use to mean any mixture of different things, a hodgepodge. And that's what we have here—an olio of words not otherwise closely related by sound or subject.

1. Hortatory (HOR-tuh-tor-ee)

This word, meaning "encouraging or intended to arouse to action," is most often used to describe a speech—often a political speech or sermon. You'll hear the same root in the verb *exhort*.

- *For good (Churchill) or bad (Hitler),* **hortatory** *speeches have made huge differences in the course of history.*

- *Good teachers and good coaches make* **hortatory** *talks, although the styles may be quite different.*

2. Chthonic (THON-ik)

This adjective, describing something related to forces from the underworld, won't often come out of your mouth. (But if it does, remember the *ch* is silent.) Still, you'll impress people by knowing a word that begins with four consonants, and you'll be ready for the wise guy (or the textbook) that pulls the related word **autochthonous** on you. (Don't ask why, but the *ch* IS pronounced in this word—say au-TOK-then-us.) It means, roughly, "on native ground, originating where found," as in *autochthonous folktales*.

- *Linnell had had such a run of bad luck that she quipped, "Could **chthonic** forces be unhappy with me?"*

- *The doctors were not sure whether the blood clot on Henry's lung was **autochthonous** or whether it had traveled through the bloodstream and lodged there.*

3. Zeitgeist (ZITE-guy'st)

Different eras have different feelings about them— different spirits—much the way different people have distinct personalities. The 1920s focused on enjoying life; in the '60s, young people were pushing for changes in attitudes toward war and the environment. *Zeitgeist,* the German word for "spirit of the time," will give you a name for such a prevailing attitude and outlook.

- *Is the popularity of the young candidate a cause of the current **zeitgeist** or a result of it?*

- *Willy Loman's aspirations to be a successful sales-man were typical of the post-World War II **zeitgeist;** his goals were to pay off the mortgage on his house, support his wife and family, and bring up two sons.*

4. Weltanschauung (VELT-un-schow-ung)

It may be a little tricky to pronounce, but this word is useful in dealing with how people think, act, and react. Literally the German word meaning "worldview," this noun gives an overall perspective on the way a person or group sees the world and interprets behavior and events.

- *The **weltanschauung** just after 9/11 was colored by outrage and fear.*

- *"If we all lived by the **weltanschauung** of today's teenagers," reflected the professor of popular culture, "love, friendship, and even religion could be determined by the Internet."*

5. Prolix (pro-LIX)

More often used to describe writing than speaking, this adjective describes a wordiness of manner, a pouring forth of too many words, too many phrases. Unlike *glib*, however, this adjective carries no suggestion of insincerity.

- *A professional editor was hired to boil down the **prolix** manuscript to a reasonable length and thus make it more appealing to publishers.*

- *"I am fascinated by the decline and fall of the Roman Empire," said Adam, "but I wish Edward Gibbon were not quite so **prolix**."*

6. Glabrous (GLAH-bruss)

Although often used in the sciences, this word can be useful outside of science, and fun. It means "bald, smooth, devoid of any projections or irregularities."

- *At the reunion, I hardly recognized my formerly hairy, bearded, and athletic friend Harold, now of the **glabrous** scalp and rotund middle.*

- *The botanist pointed out the **glabrous** leaves and stalk of the shiny plant.*

*Willy Loman's aspirations to be a successful salesman were typical of the post–World War II **zeitgeist**; his goals were to pay off the mortgage on his house, support his wife and family, and bring up two sons.*

7. Prosaic (pro-ZAY-ik)

Perhaps because this adjective comes from the Latin word for "prose" rather than "poetry," it means "straightforward" or "matter-of-fact." More often, however, it has the more negative connotation of "unimaginative" or "dull."

- *Winnie's description of her visit to Washington, D.C., was so **prosaic** that George couldn't decide if he had no desire to visit that city or no desire to go anywhere with Winnie.*

- *When Gideon asked Josh to give him a description of the girl he wanted to fix him up with, Josh replied rather **prosaically**: "She's got brown hair and brown eyes and a medium build."*

8. Bête noire (BET nwahr)

Your bête noire is your nemesis, that certain person or thing that causes you the most trouble, that you most desire to avoid, to be free of. The term is French for "black beast," and it can haunt you the way the thought of a monster under the bed haunts a child.

- *I do okay with most math courses, but integral calculus is my bête noire.*

- *Time and again, Federer has found Nadal to be the bête noire standing between him and an easy romp to the title.*

9. Limerence (LIM-mer-ence)

This word is related to an intense amorous feeling. Limerence is an emotional, psychological state wherein a person feels an overwhelming, *involuntary* romantic desire for another. It's pretty close in meaning to being crazy about someone.

- *A typical character in a John Updike novel might be a man who is struck by a sudden, overwhelming feeling of limerence for a woman he has just met.*

- *In adolescents, limerence may be attributed in large part to a sudden surge of hormones.*

10. Symbiotic (sim-by-OT-ik)

From the Greek terms meaning "living together," this word describes a close and prolonged relationship of (usually) mutual benefit to people or animals involved. The noun form is **symbiosis**.

- *It's a perfectly **symbiotic** relationship—the bird eats the food fragments between the alligator's teeth, and the gator gets a free cleaning.*

- ***Symbiosis** is not always healthy—some people choose friends who will support (or at least condone) their bad habits, like overeating or drinking too much.*

Quiz #4

CATEGORY A

Match each definition on the right with the appropriate word in the column on the left.

_____ expiate	A.	split or chasm
_____ metamorphosis	B.	a complete transformation
_____ microcosm	C.	working together to benefit both individuals
_____ schism	D.	to atone for wrongdoing
_____ symbiotic	E.	a small reflection of a large whole

CATEGORY B

Select a word from the list below that best fits each of the sentences on the next page. (One sentence calls for two words.) Some words won't be used at all.

abrogated	attenuated
dionysian	epistemology
hortatory	hubris
wraith	zeitgeist

1. Those who recall pictures of half-naked people rolling in the mud at the Woodstock concert might call the _____ of the late 1960s somewhat _____.

2. Ebenezer Scrooge reformed his miserly ways after a terrifying _____ appeared to him.

3. Some people in positions of power find it difficult to maintain a strong sense of confident leadership without taking on the negative quality of _____.

4. If you read clause 12 C, you'll agree there is no doubt that you have _____ the conditions of our contract.

5. The _____ rhetoric of Stan (the Man) Johnson helped make his basketball team successful.

CATEGORY C

1. I could handle the fact that he's prosaic or that he's prolix, but not that he's both. What's upsetting this speaker?

2. Suddenly Marcia was overcome with a feeling of limerence for John, despite the fact she found him a bit of a fop. Explain.

3. Georgia's weltanschauung is doubtless shaped by prolonged endurance of the peccadilloes of her spouse. Explain.

4. I'm feeling rather enervated by the time I spent on my exegesis of the lyrics of early Beach Boys songs. Explain.

5. Prof. Nachleben dilated on her favorite topic, the transmogrification of the economy of Pequenovia, to the pleasure of some students and the disgust of others. Explain.

21 smart words

A word to the wise? Well, here we're dealing with words *about* the wise—or maybe not so wise—describing what they know and when they know it.

1. Benighted (be-NITE-ed)

Today this adjective is always used figuratively to describe a person or an argument in moral or intellectual darkness; the "night" of ignorance has descended.

- *Prejudices that today seem utterly **benighted** may once have been considered merely opinions.*

- *"Latin is not a dead language," said the esteemed Miss Elmore, "and those who call it such are themselves **benighted**."*

2. Prescient (PRESH-ee-ent or PRESH-ent)

That *pre-* (meaning "before") at the beginning gives us a good hint about the prescient person, who has an eerie ability to know things before they happen. The noun form is **prescience**.

- *Millard picks so many winning horses that I think he must be **prescient**.*

- *As they approached the darkened house, a foreboding **prescience** came over Cher.*

3. Cognizant (COG-nuh-zunt)

Someone who's cognizant is aware, fully informed. (The word may also mean "responsible for," as in "This project is under the **cognizance** of the research division.") If you watch courtroom dramas, you may hear of someone being released "on his own **recognizance**," which is the same basic idea. Occasionally you'll hear a group of discerning people referred to as "the **cognoscenti**" (cog-no-SHENT-ee), those who are "in the know."

- *Although fully **cognizant** of the danger, the graduate student lowered himself into the cave.*

- *Fools rush in where **cognizant** people fear to tread.*

4. Astute (uh-STOOT or uh-STYOOT)

If someone says you're astute, you're being told that you are not only pretty smart, but have a penetrating mind and can see clearly into complex matters. (It may also refer to products of an astute mind.)

- *Ah, that's an **astute** observation—you're very perspicacious.*

- *Raphael knew he was expected to come up with an **astute** and elegant solution to the problem, and he struggled to meet his colleagues' expectations.*

5. Obtuse (ob-TYOOS or ob-TOOS)

To say a thing (e.g., an angle, an object) is obtuse means that it's dull, not keen or sharp. And the word means much the same when applied to people.

- *In geometry, an angle of more than ninety degrees is called* **obtuse**.

- *Some of Einstein's early teachers thought he was* **obtuse**, *but how delightful it is that he turned out to be acute.*

*Intelligence is rare, and **sagacity** even rarer—a few people can see the answers, but it's a rare **sage** who sees the broader implications in every situation.*

6. Acute (uh-CUTE)

Here's another term used in geometry—it refers to a sharp angle, one of less than ninety degrees. And if used to describe a person, it means mentally sharp.

- *Man, she's* **acute**—*she answers the vocabulary questions so fast that the teacher can barely get them out of his mouth.*

- *His* **acute** *observations earned him much respect from his colleagues.*

7. Discerning (dis-SERN-ing)

A discerning person can see into things, can recognize patterns and meanings where others may fail to do so.

- *The **discerning** Hercule Poirot saw immediately that one person in the crowd was not there to enjoy the performance.*

- *Some repeat offenders are simply amoral, incapable of **discerning** what's right and what's wrong.*

8. Sagacious (suh-GAY-shus)

The sagacious person is not only wise, but also somewhat worldly—shrewd, with what people call common sense. It's related, of course, to the word **sage**, which can be an adjective meaning "wise" or a noun meaning "a wise person." The noun form is **sagacity**.

- *The **sagacious** inventor immediately saw not only the practical application of her device, but also a clever scheme for marketing it.*

- *Intelligence is rare, and **sagacity** even rarer—a few people can see the answers, but it's a rare **sage** who sees the broader implications in every situation.*

9. Acumen (ACK-you-mun or uh-KYOO-mun)

Acumen is more likely to imply practical, applicable knowledge and understanding, as opposed to the theoretical knowledge suggested by some other words in this chapter.

- *Basil's parents despaired when he dropped out of school but rejoiced when his business **acumen** began to pay off handsomely.*

- *Good men with **acumen** accumulate goods.*

10. Hebetudinous (heb-ba-TYOOD-uh-nuss)

Okay, you're right, you're not going to need this word often. But when you want to comment (humorously, of course) about something a friend says or does that might look really stupid, and make yourself look smart at the same time, here's the word you want. **Hebetude** means "deep mental lethargy, great dullness of mind."

- *You're on the dean's list but can't answer my question? My, your **hebetude** constantly amazes me.*

- *"Of course, a **hebetudinous** person such as you may not completely understand the logic of my comments," remarked Jake, his tongue firmly in his cheek.*

22 tiny words

The words in this chapter range from four to thirteen letters in length, but despite their size they all denote the small, the minute.

1. Iota (eye-OH-ta)

This noun is not only the ninth and smallest letter of the Greek alphabet, it also connotes "a very small amount." The fact that *i* and *j* were once the same gives us a different word with the same meaning: *jot*.

- *"There isn't an **iota** of truth in what you are telling me," Barney shouted at his son. "You were the last one to use the car and there was no dent in the fender when I drove it yesterday."*

- *Mrs. Rumple squeezed a **jot** of lemon into her tea and smeared a spoonful of marmalade on her scone.*

2. Scintilla (sin-TILL-ah)

This noun means "a tiny amount," such as "a trace" or a "spark." In fact, it comes from the Latin word for "spark." It's also the root of the word **scintillating**, which means "sparkling" or "fascinating."

- *"I believe I taste a **scintilla** of nutmeg in this Sonoma Valley chardonnay," said the oenologist.*

- *"There isn't a **scintilla** of kindness in my boss," whined Geoffrey. "He wouldn't let me have the day off, even though I had tickets to the opening game of the World Series."*

3. Mite (rhymes with *tight*)

As a noun, this word can mean a lot of different tiny things—a small amount of money, a small insect, a child, or even a small particle. As an adjective, it connotes "to a small degree."

- *The sixteenth-century French essayist Michel de Montaigne once said, "Man is certainly crazy. He could not make a **mite,** and he makes gods by the dozen."*

- *"Aren't you being a **mite** ridiculous?" Tammy asked. "I can't believe you are so angry at me for being only two minutes late."*

4. Soupçon (SOOP-sone)

From the Old French word for "suspicion," this noun means a "tiny amount" or "just a trace or a hint."

- *Brigitte bought a blue suit in Paris that was elegant but understated, with just a **soupçon** of sexiness in its design.*

- *Just as we can say, "I taste a hint of sugar in this iced tea," we can say, "there is a **soupçon** of cinnamon in this banana bread."*

5. **Infinitesimal** (in-fin-ih-TES-ih-mul)

Here's a six-syllable word used to speak of something very small. It describes a size or quantity that is immeasurably tiny.

- *Isn't it amazing that something as **infinitesimal** as a virus can make someone so sick?*

- *Chaos theory deals with the ways in which something **infinitesimal** can ultimately bring about a major change: the classic example involves a violent weather change that starts with a butterfly flapping its wings.*

> *Chaos theory deals with the ways in which something **infinitesimal** can ultimately bring about a major change: the classic example involves a violent weather change that starts with a butterfly flapping its wings.*

6. **Lilliputian** (lil-ee-PU-shun)

This synonym for "very small" derives from a nation of people around six inches tall imagined by Jonathan Swift in his classic book *Gulliver's Travels*. Even the sounds in the word seem small! (That same volume also gave us *brobdingnagian*, meaning very large, and *Yahoo* for an ill-behaved human being.)

- *Madeline delighted in the dollhouse that her father built for her—he even filled the rooms with **Lilliputian** furniture.*

- *At four feet ten inches, Alberta felt practically **Lilliputian** when the class photographer clumsily placed her between two classmates who were over six feet tall.*

7. Diminutive (duh-MIN-u-tiv)

Deriving from the verb *diminish,* this adjective can suggest something very small. It's also the term for a suffix that can reduce the sense of the size of the original word.

- *Although Alexander Pope was, as a physical being, quite **diminutive,** he was a giant in terms of his poetic talent.*

- *"Okay, so I have only forty-eight pages of poems!" cried a frustrated Frank. "We'll use the **diminutive** and call it a poetry booklet, not a book."*

8. Niche (nitch OR neesh)

This noun can be a literal slit or crevice. Even more often, it's used for a selected figurative spot that perfectly suits an individual or a situation.

- *Owen marveled that the garden snake could slither into the narrow **niche** between stones of the front steps.*

- *Unless you ride a motorcycle, you may not think often about products designed and marketed especially for motorcyclists, but it's an expanding **niche** market.*

9. Minuscule (MIN-us-kyool)

From the French, this adjective originally meant "a small, as opposed to capital, letter," but it is generally used now to mean "very small, tiny." Remember the correct spelling by thinking *minus*—not *mini*.

- *The doctors discovered **minuscule** traces of mercury in the preservative used for the vaccinations but determined that they were not harmful.*

- *While she was in Venice, Laura purchased a collection of **minuscule** glass animals that she now displays on a mirrored shelf on her bedroom wall.*

10. Shard (rhymes with *lard*)

This noun most often refers to a piece of broken pottery or a fragment of any brittle material, but it can also be used to mean "a small piece," usually larger than the tiny mite, iota, or scintilla.

- *The archeologists working outside of the kibbutz in the Sahara Desert found hundreds of **shards** of pottery piled in one area of the dig, leading them to believe that they had come upon an ancient wine cellar or food pantry.*

- *After he lost his job, his home, and his wife, Frank knew that he had no choice but to pick up the **shards** of his broken life, move to a new city, and start fresh.*

23 uncertain words

Who's there? Is it a bush or a bear? Do my eyes deceive me? Are you wearing a mask? Why are things so different now?

The questions above hint at just a few of the causes of uncertainty in our world. Many words in our language attempt to express, perhaps uncertainly, some of the varieties and causes of ambiguity.

1. Indeterminacy (in-de-TUR-min-a-see)

This noun, which has grown in scholarly usage in the last few decades, captures the idea of the impossibility of being certain about things.

- *Indeterminacy* *is the ruling force in Shakespeare's* Hamlet: *Not only do we lack certainty of the title character's motives and emotions, we don't even know how old he is.*

- *Perhaps puns intrigue us because they reinforce our awareness of the basic* **indeterminacy** *of all language.*

2. Mercurial (mer-CURE-ee-ul)

The Roman god Mercury was the messenger of the gods and as such had to be very swift. So his name has been given to the chemical element mercury, which changes shape very rapidly, and to the adjective *mercurial,* used to describe someone whose moods change very rapidly. (If you've read *Romeo and Juliet,* think of Mercutio, who is certainly mercurial.) A synonym would be *volatile,* which comes from a root meaning "flying."

- *Shakespeare's character Hamlet is very **mercurial**: one minute he's very gloomy and the next he's wisecracking with old chums.*

- *George's **mercurial** nature can make him fun to be around for a while, but sometimes you want him to be a little more laid-back.*

3. Casuistry (KAZH-yoo-us-tree)

This noun refers to a subtle kind of reasoning that is designed to conceal the fact that it is deliberately misleading us. A **casuist** is one who engages in such practices. You'll sometimes see the synonym *jesuitical* (jez-u-IT-ih-kul), from the alleged use of such super subtle reasoning by the order of the Jesuits.

- *Jed had always associated the concept of **casuistry** with learned tomes of philosophy, but he came to realize the slick used car salesman who sold him a lemon possessed it in great quantity.*

- *There's no deceiver like a self-deceiver; those who cannot detect their own **casuistry** may need to have it pointed out to them.*

4. Factitious (fak-TISH-us)

This adjective describes something *lacking* in authenticity, so don't be fooled by the fact that the first syllable is *fact*.

- *Jim Dixon moved from his seat on the stage to the podium with **factitious** ease.*

- *He was terrified about giving this speech on Merrye Olde England, a subject dear to his boss's heart but a concept he himself found **factitious**.*

5. Liminal (LIM-in-ul)

Neither high nor low, neither in nor out—*liminal* describes something in between, on the edge. It comes from the Latin word meaning "threshold."

- *When the lovers in* A Midsummer Night's Dream *leave the city of Athens, they find themselves in the uncharted forest, a **liminal** area not bound by the values established by the laws of the city.*

- *Many ethical questions related to new developments in science are in a **liminal** state: many sincere people do not know what position to take.*

*The Fall of Troy was foredoomed by Fate, but each generation of inhabitants sought to postpone the **ineluctable** event.*

6. Tenebrous (TEN-eb-rus)

This adjective means dark and gloomy and is used exclusively to describe literal darkness.

- *The children looked out of the nursery window at the **tenebrous** woods behind the house and, imagining ghosts in the trees, called for their nanny.*

- *The mansion, shrouded in a **tenebrous** fog, looked like the setting for a gothic novel.*

7. Ineluctable (in-ee-LUCT-uh-bul)

This adjective is a formal word for *inevitable* or *inescapable*. In that sense, the end *is* in sight.

- *The Fall of Troy was foredoomed by Fate, but each generation of inhabitants sought to postpone the **ineluctable** event.*

- *The seductive Lola in the musical* Damn Yankees *seeks to persuade her chosen victim that struggle is meaningless, for his surrender to her is **ineluctable**.*

8. Ineffable (in-EF-a-bul)

Something ineffable cannot be expressed in words. While it may occasionally have the sense of the taboo, something forbidden, it's most often used to describe thinking about the abstract, the transcendental.

- *Poets and mystics may try to get at the **ineffable** through allusion, hint, or image.*

- *Claire's grandfather died shortly after she turned thirteen, and she found herself puzzling over ineffable* matters such as life, death, and a possible hereafter.

9. Specious (SPEE-shus)

This adjective describes things that have the ring of truth, at least on the surface, but are not entirely true. When your grandmother told you, "Beauty is only skin deep," she was warning you against specious attractiveness.

- *"If your friend told you to jump off a bridge, would you?" is a rather **specious** analogy against peer pressure. Most adolescents can tell when matters get really serious.*

- *Although Mr. Kelly was given several **specious** reasons for his dismissal, the sad truth was his employer's resentment of his creativity.*

10. Apocryphal (a-POCK-ruh-ful)

This adjective describes things of questionable truth or authenticity. (The root word, from the Greek "hidden," refers to scriptural texts accepted by some Christians, but not all.)

- *The story of George Washington and the cherry tree is **apocryphal**; he may never have come near a hatchet, but the tale illustrates a larger truth about Washington's honesty.*

- *"If it isn't true it ought to be" is another way of describing **apocryphal** tales: either they are in the spirit of truth or they are irresistibly good stories.*

24 unchanging words

These words have the sense of something that's not in a state of flux. Whether it's a cast of mind, a decree, or an oncoming force, there's not much room for argument.

1. Staid (stayed)

This adjective can be used as a compliment to mean "dignified" or, more frequently, in a negative sense, to mean "overly prim and proper."

- *Mr. Alford encouraged his eighth graders to reread Atticus Finch's **staid** but passionate defense of the judicial system in the novel* To Kill a Mockingbird.

- *The **staid** appearance of Abby and Martha, the elderly aunts in the comedy* Arsenic and Old Lace, *is indeed mere appearance, for they delight in poisoning visitors with their homemade wine.*

2. Adamant (AD-ah-ment)

Since this word comes to us from the Greek for "unconquerable" and "diamond," it's no wonder it means "impervious to reason" or "stubbornly unyielding."

- *After hearing reports of terrorist threats at the airport, Belle's parents were **adamant** about her not attending the spring break party in Cancun.*

- *Although Rajneesh thought his history grade was unfair and complained to his teacher, Mr. Lombardy remained **adamant,** pointing out that his class participation was poor and his final paper was inadequately researched.*

3. Implacable (im-PLAK-ah-bul)

We're back to unyielding with this adjective. It means "unable to be appeased or mollified." The noun form is **implacability** or **implacableness**.

- *Even though Greg brought her a bouquet of roses and apologized profusely for missing her piano recital, Jessica remained **implacable**; she just couldn't forgive him for missing her big night.*

- *Fully aware of Lotta's **implacability** when she was upset or frustrated, and fearful of her having another tantrum, her mother made sure to take an extra cupcake in case Lotta dropped hers.*

4. Inexorable (in-EX-or-ah-bul)

This adjective means "relentless" or "not capable of being stopped or changed."

- *Acutely aware of the **inexorable** passage of time, Ronak shouted "Carpe diem! Live for today!"*

- *"In the end, nature is **inexorable**," said the nineteenth-century Russian novelist Ivan Turgenev. "It has no reason to hurry and, sooner or later, it takes what belongs to it."*

5. Juggernaut (JUG-er-naut)

This noun refers to any overwhelmingly powerful, unstoppable force, usually destructive. Most people today don't know that it was originally a title for a Hindu god.

- *Has the **juggernaut** of desire for instant gratification overcome the time-honored principle of working for a long-range goal?*

- *The Dyersburg Trojans had hoped to win the regional football championship this year, but the **juggernaut** force of the Union City Golden Tornadoes prevailed.*

6. Anathema (ah-NATH-eh-ma)

This noun comes to us from the Greek word that came to mean "doomed offering" or "accursed thing." Today the meaning is roughly synonymous with a strong curse, a near wish for damnation. (Oddly, its original meaning was positive—a thing set apart as an offering to the gods—but the purely negative sense is all that's left now.) The word can refer to either the curse itself or the person or thing that is cursed. In the latter case, it is not necessary to include an article when using it in a sentence.

- *To Dorothy, a confirmed luddite, the idea of spending hundreds of dollars on a laptop computer is **anathema**; she would rather use the money for a fountain pen, some fine stationery, and an antique writing desk.*

- *In the opening act of* Macbeth, *the three witches*

*gather on the heath and revel in the **anathemas*** *they have placed upon a sailor and his wife.*

7. Indefatigable (in-de-FAT-ig-a-bul)

If you're indefatigable, your energy never ends; you're incapable of becoming fatigued. Lucky you!

- *Is it true that Julius Caesar was virtually **indefatigable**, dictating his observations on the Gallic Wars while riding on horseback?*

- *"Even if I were **indefatigable**, I don't want to work a sixteen-hour day," mused Frederick as he once again contemplated a career change from corporate lawyer to deep-sea diver.*

8. Fiat (FEE-at)

From the Latin for "let it be done," this noun means "an arbitrary order or decree," often authorized by the government.

- *After the students practically destroyed the football field after the game, the school administration issued a **fiat** banning the consumption of alcoholic beverages at university sporting events.*

- *The **fiat** against abortion drove a significant number of women away from the Church.*

9. Draconian (dra-CONE-ee-an)

This adjective describes treatment that is seen as exceedingly harsh or severe. The severe legal code of Draco, a seventh-century BC Athenian politician, is here memorialized; no dragons are involved.

- *Georgia knew she had violated the curfew her parents had set for her, but she still felt that grounding her for a month was a **draconian** punishment.*

- *Those who believe strongly in the right to bear arms will probably judge gun laws in the United Kingdom to be **draconian.***

10. Peremptory (per-EMP-tuh-ree)

A peremptory remark puts an end to debate or action, not allowing contradiction or refusal. It's no surprise then that a peremptory person is "offensively self-assured." (Don't be confused if you sometimes spot a similar-looking adjective *preemptory*. It occasionally sneaks into the language in place of the preferred form *preemptive*, as in, "Biggles made a preemptive bid for the property, an offer so good that would-be competitors retreated.")

- *The headmaster took a **peremptory** tone with the students who had missed too many classes. "Anyone who misses more than ten classes cannot graduate," he averred. "That's the rule and we're going to stick to it. There are no excuses."*

- *When Dara asked her mother whether she could stay out past her normal curfew on a school night, her mother replied with a **peremptory** "No!"*

25 potpourri

It's our fifth and final mixed-bag, or potpourri (poe-puh-REE), chapter *and* the end of the book. Check out the last word and remember that we went out with a bang.

1. **Adventitious** (ad-ven-TISH-us)

This adjective sounds as if it has to do with the arrival or *advent* of something, but it doesn't. The word means "not inherent," or "coming from an external source." Another synonym is *accidental*.

- *A large, **adventitious** population of Ecuadorians has settled in central New York State, so the local school districts teach several courses in Spanish as well as in English.*

- *Truffles sometimes grow **adventitiously** in the woods beyond the Smiths' country house, enabling Hattie Smith to add a gourmet touch to her otherwise ordinary dishes.*

2. **Dyspeptic** (dis-PEP-tic)

Literally, a person suffering from indigestion, but this adjective is often used more generally for a person who is grouchy or ill-tempered.

- *Selina's doctor recommended that she see a specialist for her recurring bouts of **dyspeptic** distress.*

- *Sharing a workspace with the perpetually **dyspeptic** Oscar did not increase Elmo's pleasure in his summer job.*

3. Exiguous (ex-IG-yoo-us)

This adjective describes something that is just barely enough for the purpose. It comes from the Latin for "measured out," suggesting a measuring cup that was never overflowing.

- *When the young boy became aware of his family's **exiguous** economic circumstances, he insisted on getting after-school jobs to help as much as he could.*

- *There was an **exiguous** outcropping of grass among the rocks; otherwise, the terrain was bleak.*

4. Numinous (NOO-min-us)

This adjective means "having a supernatural presence" or "spiritually elevated." It may come from the Greek word for "to nod," as in expressing divine approval by nodding the head.

- *Dressed in a diaphanous white gown and appearing suddenly at the top of the stairs, Belle's figure took on a **numinous** appearance in the candlelight.*

- *Nature was **numinous** for the transcendental philosophers of the nineteenth century, who believed that it was only through nature that the individual could know his own soul.*

5. Solipsist (SOL-ip-sist)

The philosophical idea behind this word is that only the self has reality or the possibility of being verified. Popularly, *solipsist* is used as a rough synonym for *narcissist,* an individual who is completely focused on him- or herself. Even the root words reflect that: *solus* (Latin for "alone") plus *ipse* (Latin for "self").

- *Did you read the jazz critic who referred to John Coltrane's playing as "**solipsistic** caterwauling"? I disagree!*

- *"You exist only because I believe you do," said Ricky to Avery, before adding, "Just kidding! I'm not really that much of a **solipsist!**"*

*George Orwell's frightening novel 1984 shows the values of the controlling party being constantly **inculcated** in citizens through both propaganda and brutalization.*

6. Inculcate (in-KULL-kate)

This verb refers to teaching, the passing on of knowledge or of values. Its etymology is startling. Since it sounds so much like the cozy word *incubate*, we might expect a warm and fuzzy kind of origin, but no. This word originated from the Latin word for "heel" with the implication of "trampling on," "grinding down." A cautionary note for all of us who are or will be teachers and/or parents!

- *Ursula hopes to **inculcate** the values of the family religion in her children not through lecturing about them but by living them.*

- *George Orwell's frightening novel 1984 shows the values of the controlling party being constantly **inculcated** in citizens through both propaganda and brutalization.*

7. Philistine (FIL-us-teen)

This noun is now used to denote a boor, a person lacking in refinement and culture. (As one dictionary wryly notes, "It has never been good to be a Philistine." In its capitalized historical form, the Philistines were the enemies of the Israelites. Few people have Goliath or Delilah on their list of "good guys.")

- *Turning down my offer of tickets to the Mahler concert, Hank smilingly said, "I'll be watching TV; you know I'm a complete **philistine**."*

- *In university towns in the medieval period, dissension between the college students and residents of the village was frequent: stereotypes of "snob" and "**philistine**" abounded in these "town-gown" conflicts.*

8. Shibboleth (SHIB-e-leth)

This noun refers to a password or a distinctive pronunciation that shows that a person is or is not an "insider," a person deserving of the name of that group. (The word comes from a passage in the Hebrew scriptures: two tribes were distinguished by the inability of one to give the correct pronunciation of *shibboleth*.)

Today the word is also used in a looser sense for a distinctive trait of a certain group.

- *The World War II film depicted the dazed Sgt. Pritchett desperately trying to recall the piece of baseball trivia that was the **shibboleth** of his unit. Without it, his comrades might think him a spy.*

- *The ease with which profane or obscene language is used in public may be the **shibboleth** of generational difference; older folk grew up with a taboo on so-called four-letter words.*

9. Sobriquet (so-bri-KAY)

This synonym for a nickname or an epithet comes straight from French where, patronizingly enough, it once meant "to chuck under the chin."

- *Mr. Hanly's extensive vocabulary prompted his students to coin the admiring **sobriquet** "The Walking Dictionary."*

- *"The Great Cham" is a **sobriquet** used variously for the Khan of the Tartary region in Asia and for the eighteenth-century writer and dictionary maker Samuel Johnson.*

10. Pyrotechnics (PY-ro-TECK-nicks)

This noun, taken literally, is the technical term for fireworks (*pyre* equals "fire" in Greek). It can also be used for a display of wit or brilliance in the performing arts that might rival the sparkling effect of skyborne rockets and Catherine wheels on the Fourth of July.

- *The verbal **pyrotechnics** in Oscar Wilde's plays are a delight for any lover of language.*

- *Doc Watson's uniqueness as a performer of traditional American folk songs comes from the beauty and grace of his style rather than from technical **pyrotechnics**.*

Quiz #5

CATEGORY A

Match each definition on the right with the appropriate word in the column on the left.

_____ benighted   A. small amount, trace

_____ shard   B. artificial, unnatural

_____ soupçon   C. a broken-off piece, fragment

_____ specious   D. unenlightened, ignorant

_____ factitious   E. sounding true, but false

CATEGORY B

Select a word from the list below that best fits each of the sentences on the next page. (One sentence calls for two words.) Some words won't be used at all.

cognizant	**dyspeptic**
implacable	**indefatigable**
ineluctable	**mercurial**
niche	**shibboleth**
sobriquet	

1. She soaks up new vocabulary terms like a sponge; her _____ should be "the word-bird."

2. Now she's an English teacher, so I guess she's found her _____.

3. Some people think we're destined for a given career, that we move toward it as to a/an _____ fate.

4. I'd be _____ and exhausted after grading all those irritating themes, but she's _____; she just keeps going.

5. She's kind, but sometimes unforgiving—if she catches someone cheating, she's _____.

CATEGORY C

1. Brian said that the speaker's remarks showed considerable acumen, and that she had a sagacious mind. What, specifically, does Brian think of the speaker?

2. Martha observed that her cousin was trying to inculcate the values of a philistine into the youngsters. Does Martha approve of her cousin's practices? Why or why not?

3. It was difficult for Gary to get his mind around the concept of solipsism. What is solipsism, and why might it be difficult to understand?

4. The teacher's peremptory comments about extra homework for hebetudinous students seemed a bit draconian. Explain.

5. He felt a scintilla of dread on seeing the deserted old church in the woods; as he entered, however, a strong sense of the numinous overtook him. Explain.

appendix: quiz answers

Quiz #1

CATEGORY A

C

D

A

E

B

CATEGORY B

1. temerity

2. anomie

3. lacerated

4. pubescent

5. truculent

CATEGORY C

1. If I met a feckless jingoist, I'd run fast. Who wants to be around an irresponsible person who's a rabid supporter of rushing to war?

2. Maybe, just maybe you could laugh at the dark humor of the sardonic nature of the criticism, but no one could benefit from being cut down as scathing criticism would do to you.

3. This speech would be very unpleasant to listen to. A ranting speech that rips colleagues to shreds. No thanks.

4. Usually a bellicose or warlike state would most likely fill citizens with energy to support (or oppose) the war. But it's possible that it might make some feel powerless, feel a sense of lassitude, in such a circumstance.

5. This tangled situation may seem really funny some day, but right now it's understandable that it's making you irritable.

Quiz #2

CATEGORY A

D

B

A

E

C

CATEGORY B

1. callipygian

2. obfuscation

3. brio

4. mountebank

5. didactic

CATEGORY C

1. This is a big disagreement because you think you're being wise and I say you're not taking things seriously enough.

2. This sounds like a wonderful person: he's very knowledgeable but he's also sensitive to shades of meaning in human relationships.

3. Okay, do you want to sit with your head and hands imprisoned, or do you want to listen to recordings of stomach rumblings? I'd pick the latter; after all, whale songs once became popular.

4. Having the power of reasoning is good, but doryphores turn this asset to a negative with their annoying pointing out of small errors.

5. Most people in a shady grove full of lovely trees would pick the company of someone in a carefree (insouciant) mood. But you could make an argument for an outdoor setting enhancing an intellectual discussion with your very knowledgeable friend, the polymath.

Quiz #3

CATEGORY A

C

E

A

B

D

CATEGORY B

1. paradox

2. oxymoron

3. impunity, recidivist

4. doppelganger

5. redundant

CATEGORY C

1. He'd be a very bossy boss, demanding and dictatorial. She would nag and scold him, treating him much the way he treated his employees.

2. That they are insignificant, of little or no value in improving the draft.

3. He may appear to be a buttoned-down, go-along rule-follower, but under that thin surface layer (patina), there lives a rule-breaker who disregards tradition.

4. As he readied himself to face the rival who's most threatening to him, he wouldn't say much about intellectual analysis but a lot about his gut feeling.

5. He revised them, replacing "bad" words with those he considered more appropriate.

Quiz #4

CATEGORY A

D

B

E

A

C

CATEGORY B

1. zeitgeist, dionysian

2. wraith

3. hubris

4. abrogated

5. hortatory

CATEGORY C

1. You could handle his being dull OR wordy but dull AND wordy is just too much!

2. Despite John's affectation of velvet jackets and watch fobs, Marcia is feeling a sense of irrational attraction and longing for him.

3. If Georgia's husband continually commits small transgressions, we're not surprised that she sees the world as a bit dark and gloomy.

4. Giving a scholarly unpacking (exegesis) of lines like "Fun, fun, fun in the California sun" can certainly rob one of all energy.

5. Professor Nachleben must know a lot of that complete change in Pequenovia, and we hope she has an interesting manner as she talks expansively about it.

Quiz #5

CATEGORY A

D

C

A

E

B

CATEGORY B

1. sobriquet

2. niche

3. ineluctable

4. dyspeptic, indefatigable

5. implacable

CATEGORY C

1. He thinks she's very wise, and has a keen insight.

2. She most definitely does not. She thinks he's trying to instill in them the values of a smug (often middle-class) person who has no appreciation for the arts, and who may well be against them.

3. It's the belief that the self is the only thing that really exists (or at least, the only thing that can be proven to exist). He might wonder, if he's the only thing in existence, what to make of all the other things and people, apparently very real.

4. Her comments were issued as commands, leaving no room for argument. Hebetudinous students are the least bright, and draconian means very harsh.

5. A scintilla is a tiny bit (a spark), and a numinous feeling is spiritual, mystical.

about the authors

Edward B. Fiske served for seventeen years as education editor of the *New York Times*, and he is the author of *Fiske Guide to Colleges* and numerous other books on college admissions. Jane Mallison has taught for more than twenty years and has served on the College Board SAT Committee. David Hatcher has written and co-written several books, workbooks, and other training materials on vocabulary, writing, proofreading and editing, and related subjects. His writing has been published in the *Washington Post* and in national magazines. Jane Mallison and David Hatcher have MA degrees from, respectively, Duke University and Indiana University. This is their first collaboration since their joint journalistic efforts as undergraduates.